# A Taste of Zanzibar
## CHAKULA KIZURI

# A Taste of Zanzibar

## CHAKULA KIZURI

**Swahili Recipes by Zarina Jafferji**

**With an introduction by Bethan Rees Jones**

**Photographs by Javed Jafferji and Phillip Waterman**

The Gallery Publications

**Previous Pages:**
Zanzibar coffee served with halwa

**Right:**
Papaya and lime juice, Exotic fruit drink
Tamarind juice

**Next Page:**
Fried fish with salad

**Left:**
Fried vermicelli

**Next Page:**
Vitumbua and Mkate wa kumimina

First published in 2002
Revised and updated in 2005  by
The Gallery Publications
P.O. Box 3181, Zanzibar
email: gallery@swahilicoast.com

© The Gallery Publications
Recipes by Zarina Jafferji
Introduction and editing by Bethan Rees Jones
Revised edition updated by Judi Palmer
Photographs by © Javed Jafferji and Phillip Waterman

ISBN 9978 667 02 3

*Acknowlegments*

This book is dedicated to the memory of Ummul Mumineen Busaheba Amatulla Aisaheba.

I owe a debt of gratitude to my late mother Huseinabai Jafferji for awakening my interest in cooking.

I would like to thank my family and friends for their creative ideas and invaluable contributions to the preparation of this project.

A great deal of time has been  dedicated to putting the recipes in writing. I am grateful to all the people who encouraged me to complete the book for the new millennium, specially Abid Jafferji, Javed Jafferji and my sister Zehra for her patience and for putting up with mess I made in the kitchen.

I would also like to thank the following for their contribution. Bethan Rees Jones who wrote the introduction and proof-read the manuscript; Javed Jafferji and Philip Waterman, for their photography; Phylis Delord, Mwajuma Maulid, and Nana Ameir for their initial assessment of the first draft and Bashira Jafferji for her contribution of the recipes of the exotic drinks of Zanzibar.

Last but not least, Highgate Stationers and Printers for allowing me to use their computer resources, and Amir Chomoko for helping with computer related issues.

# Contents

| | |
|---|---|
| Introduction | 15 |
| Glossary | 19 |
| Glossary in different languages | 23 |
| Hot & Cold Drinks | 25 |
| Soups and Appetisers | 31 |
| Seafood | 37 |
| Chicken & Meat dishes | 45 |
| Vegetarian Dishes | 51 |
| Sensational Savouries | 59 |
| Sweet Snacks | 71 |
| Rice Dishes | 75 |
| Desserts | 81 |
| Bread | 89 |
| Sauces, Relishes and Pickles | 91 |
| Index | 95 |

**Left from top:** Lentil Bhajia and coconut chutney, Prawn pilau and Tandoori Chicken.

# Introduction

Known as the Spice Island, it should come as no surprise that Zanzibari food and cooking offer an exotic array of aromas and flavours. Set a few degrees south of the equator, Zanzibar luxuriates in the myriad shades of green found in the tropics. Long renowned for its fertility and situated in the azure seas of the Indian Ocean, Zanzibar used to command a key position as an entrepot to the African interior. For centuries trading dhows arrived with the monsoon winds, connecting the islands to Arabia and the Gulf and many Zanzibari dishes reveal these different influences - linking Africa with Arabic coffee, Indian curries, Goan masalas, all of which form a part of Zanzibari cooking today. Cloves still perfume the air and a hint of the island's colourful history can be tasted in the recipes of typical Zanzibari dishes.

The trade over the centuries, as well as successive colonial powers, have left their mark both on the cuisine and the topography of Zanzibar and Pemba islands. Different fruits, vegetables and spices were introduced and those that flourished in the tropical climate were soon incorporated into Zanzibari life. During the seventeenth century, the Portuguese introduced food crops gathered on earlier voyages of discovery, such as maize, cassava, cashew and jojoba trees, avocado and guava as well as the word for pineapple - *nanasi*. Cloves, which were to become the islands' most important cash crop, were introduced from Mauritius by the Omani Arabs who ruled as sultans from the early 1800s until 1964. The Omanis were enticed by Zanzibar's lush fertility and they began to clear and cultivate the western part of the island, developing large and prosperous plantations farmed by slaves. The islands became known as *al khudra* - the green islands. The profits from the clove harvest may have declined in recent years but they are still an important ingredient in dishes such as *pilau* or *biriani* and they are used in local medicine to relieve toothache and stomach problems.

Palm trees fringe the islands and provide one of the key ingredients for Zanzibari cooking - the coconut. It may take up to 10 years for a palm to bear fruit and in Zanzibar every part of the palm tree is used. Young, green coconuts are drunk; coconut oil is used in cooking and as a hair and body moisturiser. The leaves are used

**Left:** Zanzibar lobster

# Glossary

**Bay leaves:**
An aromatic herb with preservative properties used either fresh or dried for flavouring curry and rice dishes and not meant to be eaten.

**Cardamom:**
Cardamom is a small oval, green or white (bleached) pod containing several small black highly aromatic seeds. Its culinary uses include desserts and cakes as well as pilau and meat dishes. It can be used with or without pods.

**Cassava:**
Cassava is a staple part of the diet in many African countries, the West Indies and Brazil. Cassava is an edible tuberous root which is full of starch. It is cooked whole or pounded to a pulp or granular powder. In Zanzibar this ground form is known as 'ugali'.

**Chilli:**
A hot fiercely flavoured pepper which turns bright red when ripe. Chilli powder is made from dried red chillies. Green (fresh) chillies are frequently used.

**Cinnamon:**
Cinnamon is used in stick or powdered form in rice and curry dishes, sweets and cakes. The sticks are just used for their aroma and flavour and are not meant to be eaten.

**Cloves:**
Cloves are the main cash crop of Zanzibar and Pemba. Cloves are aromatic and a very powerful antiseptic. They are used whole or in powdered form in rice and curry dishes, sweets and cakes.

**Coconut milk:**
An essential ingredient in Zanzibari cuisine and most Zanzibari dishes are cooked in coconut milk. Here are simple ways to prepare it. Break a fresh coconut into two halves and grate the flesh on a hand grater or put the flesh into an electric blender or food processor with a little water and blend until it is very finely grated. Add 3 cups of water to 2 cups of freshly grated coconut and squeeze the milk from the flesh of the coconut with your hands and strain through a muslin lined sieve. The first extraction of milk is called thick milk. For the second extraction add 2 cups of warm water to the same grated coconut. Squeeze and strain the milk again to obtain thin coconut milk.

Solidified creamed coconut is available in packets which can be dissolved in hot water and brought slowly to the boil. Powdered coconut is also available in packets. It is easiest to use creamed coconut which is sold in firm white blocks (in 7oz - 198g packets).

**Coriander:**
These are round seeds often used ground or crushed, sometimes mixed with cumin to form the masala for curry.

**Coriander leaves:**
They are used for garnishing and flavouring as an aromatic herb similar to parsley.

**Cumin seeds:**
These are tiny greyish seeds resembling the caraway family. Freshly roasted and ground cumin has a wonderful aroma and adds a rich flavour to food. These can be used whole or in powdered form.

**Curry leaves:**
Aromatic leaves used to flavour curry. They are usually not eaten.

**Clockwise from top left:**
Cinnamon, Black pepper, Coriander, Cardamom, Vanilla, and Saffron,

and

**Dhal:**

A type of lentil.

**Garam masala :**

This is an aromatic mixture of spices which varies in hotness from cook to cook. Garam masala is not a standardised mixture of spices and varies between different regions. A Zanzibari recipe is as follows:

1/2 oz cardamom pods

4 oz cumin seeds

4 oz coriander

2 oz turmeric

2 oz cinnamon sticks

2 oz cloves

2 oz ginger (dry)

2 oz black peppercorns

1/2 oz mace (optional)

**Method**

Roast all the ingredients on a low heat for 5 to 6 minutes and grind them in a coffee grinder. Store in an airtight jar and the spices will keep for two months.

**Garlic :**

Garlic is a natural antibiotic and a blood cleanser. It is a strong smelling bulb with segments known as cloves used in curry and chutney. It is available in powdered or paste form which can be stored in the refrigerator. To grind garlic into a paste, blend the segments in a food processor with a little water and some salt.

**Ginger (fresh) :**

This light brown root is used chopped, grated or as a paste. It needs to be peeled before it is chopped, grated or made into a paste and it can be stored in the refrigerator. To grind ginger into a paste, chop it coarsely first and blend in a food processor with a little water and some salt.

**Ginger - dry ground :**

This is dried and powdered and can be used in drinks and bread.

**Gram flour :**

This is flour made from chickpeas. It is used for making savoury and sweet dishes.

**Jaggery :**

Compacted unrefined hard brown sugar made from the palmyra palm.

**Lemon grass :**

Lemon grass has a strong lemony smell and taste and is used fresh or dried in fish dishes, soups, tea and cold drinks.

**Mace :**

The outer membrane of nutmeg which is used for flavouring curry and fish dishes.

**Nutmeg :**

The nutmeg is a single seed which looks like a small apricot. The nutmeg is the dark brown dried kernel of this seed. It is widely used in desserts, cakes and meat dishes.

**Mint :**

An aromatic herb used in raita, chutney, snacks and as a garnish.

**Mustard seeds :**

These round black seeds are used to flavour vegetable and other dishes. Scatter them into hot oil and they will turn deliciously nutty. Coarsely ground mustard seeds are used in pickles.

**Pepper-black :**

Green peppercorns are sun dried until they turn hard and black. Use whole peppercorns to flavour stock and cooking liquids. Ground black pepper can be used for spice mixtures or marinades.

**Saffron :**

Saffron is the most expensive spice and is used as a flavouring and colour in biriani, pilau, meat and sweet dishes. It is also available in powdered form.

### Sugar syrup :

For various sweets, different kinds of sugar syrup are required and the strength is measured by strings. Boil sugar and water for a few minutes and check with a drop between thumb and forefinger. Press thumb and forefinger together and see if the syrup forms a string. If two or more strings form, then the syrup will be thicker.

### Sesame seeds :

Sesame seeds are rich in oil and have a wonderful nutty flavour especially after they have been roasted. They are used in bread, naan, confectionery, salads and savoury dishes.

### Tamarind :

Tamarind is a sticky dark brown velvety fruit. It has a hard dry outer shell which is discarded. The fruit is soaked in water to extract its juice and this can be used in curry as a souring agent. Adds piquancy to relishes, makes the base for chutney, sauces and also cold drinks.

### Turmeric :

A root spice which has a distinct yellow colour and is used in savoury dishes such as dhal, curry, rice and many other dishes to give colour and a pungent flavour. It has antiseptic value.

### Vanilla :

The vanilla pod is a blackish brown capsule about 4 inches long which belongs to the climbing orchid family. It is used as a principal flavouring agent in Zanzibari food and the aroma is subtle and delicate.

## Glossary in different languages :

| English | Kiswahili | Indian | Italian | French | German |
|---------|-----------|--------|---------|--------|--------|
| Bay leaves | Mjani /Mdalasini | Taj patta | Alloro | Laurier | Lorbeer blatt |
| Bread Fruit | Shelisheli | Bread Fruit | Frutto del pane | Fruit a pain | Brotfrucht |
| Cardamom | Hiliki | Elaichi | Cardamomo | Cardamone | Kardam |
| Cassava | Muhogo | Cassava | Cassava/Manioca | Manioc | Manioka |
| Chilli | Pilipili | Lal nirchi | Peperoncino | Piment | Paprikas |
| Cinnamon | Mdalasini | Tej | Cannella | Cannelle | Zimt |
| Cloves | Karafu | Lovange | Garofano | Girofle | Nelke |
| Coconut | Nazi | Narial | Noce di cocco | Noix de coco | Coconuss |
| Coconut milk | Tuwi | Tuwi | Latte di cocco | Lait de noix de coco | Coconuss Milch |
| Coriander (seeds) | Gilgilani | Dhana | Coriandolo (semi) | Coriandre (graines) | Koriander |
| Coriander (leaves) | Kothmiri | Kothmir | Corandolo (foglie) | Corandre (feuilles) | Koriander blaetten |
| Corn flour | Unga wa mahindi | Makkai ka atta | Farina di mais | Farine de mais | Korn Mehl |
| Cumin seeds | Uzile | Jerra | Cumino | Cumin | Kreuzkummel |
| Curry leaves | Mvuje | Kari patta | Foglie di curry | Feuilles de curry | Curry blatt |
| Garam masala | Mchanganyiko wa viungo | Garam masala | Garam masala | Melange d'epices | Gemischte gevuerze |
| Garlic | Kitungu thom | Lasan | Aglio | Ail | Knoblauch |
| Ginger fresh | Tangawizi mbichi | Adrak | Zenzero (fresco) | Racine de galgant | Ingwer (frisch) |
| Dried ginger | Tangawizi kavu | Sooth | Zenzero (essicato) | Gingembre | Ingwer |
| Gram flour | Unga wa dengu | Besen | | | |
| Green Banana | Ndizi mbichi | Green banana | Banana verde | Banane verte | Gruene Banane |
| Jaggery | Sukari guru | Gour | Melassa | Melasse | Jagrezucker |
| Lemon grass | Mchaichai | Neem patta | Erba di limone | Citronelle | Zitronengras |
| Mace | Basibasi | Javantri | | Macis | Muskabluete |
| Nutmeg | Khungu Manga | Jaifar | Noce moscata | Muscade | Muskatnusse |
| Mint | Nanaa | Fudino | Menta | Menthe | Pfeffermuenze |
| Mustard | Haradali (rai) | Rai | Senape | Moutarde | Senf |
| Papaya | Papai | Papaya | Papaia | Papaye | Papaia |
| Pepper(black) | Pilipili manga | Miri | Pepe | Poivre noir | Schwarz Pfeffer |
| Saffron | Zafrani | Kesar | Zafferano | Safran | Safran |
| Sugar syrup | Shira | Chasni | Sciroppo di zucchero | Sirop de sucre | Zucker sirup |
| Salt | Chumvi | Neemak | Sale di cucina | Sel | Kochsalz |
| Sesame seeds | Ufuta | Tal | Sesamo (semi) | Sesame (graine) | Sesam (koerner) |
| Sweet banana | Ndizi mbivu | Plantain | Banana dolce | Banane douce | Suesse Banane |
| Sweet Potato | Kiazi kitamu | Sweet Potato | Patata dolce | Patate douce | Suesse Kartoffel |
| Tamarind | Ukwaju | Amli | Tamarindo | Tamarine | Tamarind |
| Turmeric | Manjano | Haldi | Curcuma | Safran des Indes | Kurkuma |
| Vanilla | Vanilla | Vanilla | Vaniglia | Vanille | Vanille |
| Wheat | Ngano | Ghav | Farina di frumento | Farine | Weizen |

**Left:** Turmeric, Ground coriander, Chilli powder, Salt, Ground cardamom and Garam masala.

# Hot & Cold Drinks

### Zanzibar coffee (Kahawa)

Serves 6 people

**Ingredients**

3 cups water

3 cardamom pods

6 tsps freshly ground coffee

1/2 tsp ground ginger

1/2 tsp ground cardamom

**Method**

Boil the water for 10 minutes with the cardamom pods. Add the coffee and boil for a further 5 minutes. Lastly add the ginger and cardamom powder and serve piping hot in small cups.

### Hot ginger drink (Tangawizi)

Serves 6 people

This is soothing and is very good for colds and flu.

**Ingredients**

4 cups water

3 tsps ground ginger

sugar to taste

**Method**

Bring water to the boil. Add the ginger and sugar to taste and boil for a further 5 minutes. Serve piping hot in small cups.

### Zanzibar Spiced Tea (Chai ya viungo)

Serves 6 people

This is an commonly drunk in Zanzibar and is definitely worth trying.

**Ingredients**

4 oz small cardamon pods

2 oz dry ginger

2 oz black peppercorns

2 oz cloves

2 oz cinnamon

2 oz pcs nutmeg

Raost all the ingredients on a low heat for 10-15 minutes or until crisp. Allow to cool then grind in a grinder. Store this tea masala powder in an air tight jar.

**Method**

Make black tea adding 1tsp of tea masala and sugar to taste and let it simmer for a few minutes. strain and serve hot. Milk is optional.

### Tamarind juice (Maji ya ukwaju)

Serves 6 people

A tropical juice.

**Ingredients**

4 cups of water

1/2 lb tamarind pods

2 cups sugar

1 small piece jaggery (optional)

**Method**

Soak the tamarind for 1 hour in 4 cups of water, then boil it. When cool, blend the mixture and strain it. Add 2 cups of sugar, the jaggery and boil again for 5 to 10 minutes. Taste and if necessary add some more sugar. Serve very chilled.

### Papaya and lime juice (Maji ya papai na ndimu)

Serves 2 people

A simple and delicious drink.

**Ingredients**

1 medium papaya peeled and seeded

juice of 1 lime

sugar to taste

pinch of salt

crushed ice

**Method**

Blend all the ingredients until smooth. Serve with crushed ice and garnish with a slice of lemon.

**Left:** Arabic coffee pot and cups used to serve Zanzibar coffee.

## Lemon grass tea (Mchai chai)

Serves 6 people

This is an excellent palate cleanser after a meal.

**Ingredients**

3 cups water

Lemon grass

sugar to taste

lemon juice to taste

**Method**

Bring water to the boil, add the lemon grass and allow to brew for a while depending on how strong you like tea. Add sugar to taste and serve hot in small cups. Or make black tea, adding some lemon grass and allow to brew for a few minutes. Add sugar and lemon juice to taste. Strain and serve hot in small cups. milk is optional.

## Orange and mango juice (Maji ya machungwa na nyembe)

Serves 2 people

A delicious juice to melt the taste buds.

**Ingredients**

1 cup of orange juice

1 large mango peeled and seeded

juice of 1 lemon

sugar to taste

pinch of salt

crushed ice

slices of lemon or mint

**Method**

Blend all the ingredients until smooth. Serve with crushed ice and garnish with a slice of lemon or mint.

## Fruity coconut drink (Maji ya matunda na nazi)

Serves 4 people

Surprise your guests!

**Ingredients**

1 banana

1 medium pineapple

1 cup pineapple juice

1/2 cup coconut milk

1/2 cup crushed ice

1 scoop ice cream

few drops of red syrup

**Method**

Cut two small wedges from the pineapple and keep aside for garnishing. Peel and chop the remaining pineapple and blend with the banana and pineapple juice to a smooth puree and add water if necessary. Add the ice cream to the blender. Slowly pour in the coconut milk and then add the crushed ice and process until smooth. Divide the drink mixture between four glasses. Trickle the red syrup over the top of the drink to give a slight pinkish effect. Garnish with a slit pineapple wedge on the rim of each glass and serve with a drinking straw.

## Passion fruit juice (Maji ya passion)

Serves 6 people

**Ingredients**

1 1b passion fruit

1/2 1b sugar or to taste

pinch of salt

5 cups water

**Method**

Blend the pulp of the passion fruit with all the ingredients. Strain and refrigerate. Serve with crushed ice.

## Guava juice (Sherbati ya mapera)

Serves 6-8 people

**Ingredients**

4-5 medium guava

1 cup sugar or to taste

6 cups water

juice of 1 lemon

**Method**

Blend the guava with all the ingredients. Strain and refrigerate. Serve with crushed ice.

**Left:** Lemon grass tea

## Bungo juice (Rubber vine) (Maji ya bungo)

Serves 6 people

The roughly spherical, orange-green fruits are the source of a wonderfully fluorescent-orange juice which is tart and refreshing.

**Ingredients**

2 bungo fruits

2 cups sugar

6 cups water

pinch of salt

**Method**

Cut the bungo in half and remove all the seeds. Soak the seeds in water for 10-15 minutes then blend the mixture with the other ingredients. Strain and if necessary add some sugar. Serve very chilled.

## Exotic fruit drink (Maridadi sherbati)

Serves 6 people

**Ingredients**

1 cup orange juice

1 cup pineapple juice

1/2 cup passion fruit juice

1 small papaya peeled and seeded

1 cup sugar or to taste

slices of lemon and mint to garnish

pinch of salt

crushed ice

**Method**

Blend all the ingredients until smooth, Serve with crushed ice and garnish with a slice of lemon and mint.

## Marrow and mango juice (Maji ya mungunye na embe)

Serves 4 people

**Ingredients**

1 medium white marrow peeled

2 unripe mangoes, peeled and seeded

1 cup sugar or to taste

3 cups water

**Method**

Blend all the ingredients until smooth. Strain and refrigerate. Serve with crushed ice.

## Golden apple juice (Maji ya embe kizungu)

Serves 4 people

**Ingredients**

2 golden apples, peeled and seeded

1/2 cup sugar or to taste

3 cups water

**Method**

Blend all the ingredients until smooth. Strain and refrigerate. Serve with crushed ice. Garnish with mint.

## Soursop juice (Maji ya mstafeli)

Serves 4 people

**Ingredients**

1 medium soursop

1/2 cup sugar or to taste

3 cups water

a pinch of salt

**Method**

Blend the inner part of the soursop with all the ingredients. Strain and refrigerate. Serve with crushed ice.

## Rose apple juice (Maji ya matoufaa)

Serves 4 people

**Ingredients**

12 rose apples

1/2 cup sugar or to taste

juice of 1 lemon

pinch of salt

5 cups water

**Method**

Blend all the ingredients until smooth. Strain and refrigerate. Serve chilled.

**Left:** Marrow and unripe mango juice, Bungo juice and Passion fruit juice

# Soups and Appetisers

## Coconut porridge (Uji wa nazi)

Serves 4 people

This is a kind of thin savoury porridge and it is traditionally eaten during the month of Ramadhan (the fasting month).

**Ingredients**

4 tbsps rice flour

1/2 cup coconut milk

5 cups water

salt and pepper to taste

**Method**

Mix the flour and 1/2 cup of water to a smooth paste. Boil 4 cups of water and add the rice flour paste stirring continuously. Reduce the heat and simmer for 10 minutes. Add the coconut milk and cook for 5 to 7 minutes. Add salt and pepper to taste. Serve hot.

## Spicy chicken soup (supu ya kuku viungo)

Serve 4-5 people

**Ingredients**

1 lb chicken cut into small pieces

4-5 cups water

1 chicken stock cube

2 stalks lemon grass cut into small pieces

1 onion chopped

1 small piece of ginger

3 tsps lemon juice

10 mushrooms (optional)

2-3 chillies

2 stalks coriander and spring onions to garnish

**Method**

Cook the chicken in 4-5 cups of water. Add the chopped onion, ginger, lemon grass, salt and cook until the chicken is tender. Add the chicken stock cube, lemon juice, chillies and mushrooms and cook for 5 minutes. Garnish with coriander and spring onions and serve hot.

## Prawn soup (Supu ya kamba)

Serves 4 people

**Ingredients**

2 1/2 pints (1.5 Lit) stock

1 lb prawns shelled

3 stalks lemon grass chopped (optional)

3 stalks spring onions chopped

1 stalk fresh coriander chopped

1 green chillies chopped

peel of 1 lime

1 stick of cinnamon

2 cloves

2 cardamom pods

a few whole black peppercorns

salt to taste

**Method**

Put the stock and all the spices except the coriander, spring onions and chillies into a saucepan and bring to the boil. Cover and simmer for 15 minutes. Strain the liquid and add the prawns and cook for 5 minutes. Garnish with coriander, spring onions and chillies and serve hot.

## Pumpkin soup (Supu ya tango)

Serves 6-8 people

**Ingredients**

1 small pumpkin

1 1b meat with bones cut into small pieces

1 medium onion chopped

1 tsp garlic paste

3-4 tomatoes medium size, chopped

2 cups water

1/2 cup coconut milk

2 tsps oil

salt and pepper to taste

**Method**

Cut the pumpkin in half, peel and remove all the seeds cut into small pieces. Saute the onion in the oil. Add the tomatoes, meat,

**Left:** Coconut porridge

garlic, salt and pepper and cook with two cups of water until the meat is soft. Remove bones. Add coconut milk and pumpkin and simmer for another 10-15 minutes. Add hot water if necessary and simmer for a further 5 minutes.

## Fish cakes (Cutlesi ya samaki)

Serves 6 people

Any kind of white fish can be used.

### Ingredients

1 1/2 lbs fish

3 medium onions finely chopped

3 medium potatoes boiled and mashed  OR

3 slices soaked bread (squeeze out the water)

3 fresh green chillies chopped

coriander chopped

1 tbsp ginger paste

1 tbsp garlic paste

1 tsp garam masala

pinch of ground turmeric

lemon juice to taste

salt and pepper to taste

breadcrumbs

3 eggs, beaten

oil for frying

### Method

Boil the fish with a little salt. Debone the fish and put to one side. Put the next 11 ingredients in a  food processor, including the bread or potatoes and blend together.

Lastly add fish and blend for a second. Roll each spoonful into a ball and then flatten into fish cake size, coating well with breadcrumbs. Dip the fish cakes into the well beaten eggs and shallow fry over a medium heat, turning once or twice until   golden brown. Drain on kitchen paper and serve on a bed of salad.

## Fish soup (Supu ya samaki)

Serves 6 people

### Ingredients

2 medium fish

2 onion chopped

1 tsp garlic paste

2 tomatoes chopped

2 potatoes peeled and diced

2 carrots peeled and diced

1 bay leaf

1 tsp garam masala

2 tsps oil

juice of 1 lemon

1/2 cup coconut milk

4 cups water

salt and pepper to taste

### Method

Fillet the fish, separate the bones and heads and keep aside. Saute the chopped onions in the oil until soft. Add th garlic, bay leaf, fish bones and heads and bring to the boil in four cups of water for 15 minutes. Strain and discard the bones and heads. Add the chopped tomatoes, potatoes, carrots, garam masala to the stock and cook until the vegetables are tender. Add the fish fillets and cook for a further 10 minutes. Add the coconut milk and cook on a medium heat for 2 minutes. Garnish with lemon juice.

## Chicken and groundnut soup(Supu ya kuku na karanga)

Serves 4 people

You can substitute fish or prawns in this soup

### Ingredients

1 lbs chicken cut into small pieces

2 ~~5~~ cups water  chicken broth

2 ~~3~~ onions chopped

3 tomatoes chopped  (1 small can diced)

1 tsp garlic paste  (3 cloves)

1 tsp ginger paste

2 chillies chopped

2 tbsps oil     + 2 carrots diced

1/2 cup groundnut paste

salt and pepper to taste

---

**Left:** Fish cakes

**Method**

Saute the chopped onions in the oil until soft. Add the garlic ginger and tomatoes and cook for 3 minutes. Add 5 cups of water and simmer for a further 3 minutes. Add the chicken pieces, chillies, salt, pepper and groundnut paste and bring to the boil then cook for 30 minutes on a medium heat or until the chicken is cooked. Serve as a soup or with rice or ugali.

## Minced meat cutlets (Cutlesi ya nyama)

Serves 6 people

**Ingredients**

1 lb minced beef or lamb

2 medium onions finely chopped

2 slices bread, soaked in water and squeezed

1 tsp ginger paste

1 tsp garlic paste

1 tsp garam masala

1 tsp chilli powder

2 green chillies finely chopped

5 stalks coriander chopped

2-3 eggs, beaten

salt and pepper to taste

oil for frying

**Method**

Soak the bread in water for a few minutes. Squeeze out all the water and mix it thoroughly with the minced meat and all the other ingredients except the eggs. Blend the mixture just for asecond. Divide the mixture into 12 to 15 equal portions. Flatten each portion into a round shape on a breadcrumbed surface and coat them well. Dip the cutlets into the beaten eggs and shallow fry over a medium heat, turning once or twice until golden brown. Drain on kitchen paper and serve hot on a bed of salad with your choice of chutney.

## Chicken kebabs (Kababu ya kuku)

Serves 6 people

**Ingredients**

1 lb minced chicken

2 slices bread, soaked in water and squeezed

1 tsp garlic paste

1 tsp ginger paste

1 green chilli chopped

juice of 1 lemon

1 tsp black pepper

salt to taste

coriander chopped

spring onions chopped

oil for frying

**Sauce**

2 tbsps oil

2 tbsps yogurt

1 tsp red chilli powder

pinch of salt

**Method**

Mix the chicken with all the ingredients and leave for 1 hour to marinade. Divide into 12 balls and mould on to skewers. Grill over a low heat until cooked on all sides. Remove from the skewers and put aside on a bed of salad. Heat 2 tbsps of oil in a frying pan on a low heat, add the yogurt and chilli powder and a pinch of salt and cook for 1 minute. Pour the sauce over the kebabs and serve as a starter.

**Left:** Minced meat cutlets

# Seafood

Being an island, fish and seafood are never far from the Zanzibar table. The flavours of spices wonderfully enhance fish or prawn dishes.

## Fish Masala (Samaki wa salo)

Serves 6 people

**Ingredients**

2 lbs fish fillets

juice of 1 lemon

1 medium onion chopped

1 tsp garlic paste

1 tsp ginger paste

1 green chilli finely chopped

1 tbsp garam masala

1 tbsp tomato puree

1/2 cup oil for frying

salt and pepper to taste

chopped coriander to garnish

**Method**

Marinade the fish in the salt, pepper and lemon juice for at least 1-2 hours. Heat the oil and fry the chopped onions until translucent. Add all the spices and cook together until well blended over a medium heat. Drain the marinade from the fish and fry it in 1/2 cup of oil until brown. Put the fried fish on a baking tray and pour the cooked sauce over the fish and bake in the oven for 10 minutes at a moderate heat. Lastly garnish with mace, chopped coriander and serve hot with spicy potatoes and rice.

## Fish in coconut (Samaki ya kupaka)

Serves 6 people

Coconut gives this dish an exotic touch.

**Ingredients**

2 lbs white fish

1 1bs garlic paste

2 green chillies chopped

juice of 1 large lemon

1 medium onion chopped

1 medium tomato skinned and chopped

2 1/2 cups thick coconut milk

2 tbsps oil

salt and pepper to taste

a few stalks of chopped corriander

**Method**

Mix the garlic, salt, pepper and lemon juice and marinade the fish for at least 2 hours. Oil the baking dish and bake the fish lightly. Puree the onions, chillis, tomatoes and coriander in a blender. Take 2 tbsps of oil and fry the pureed mixture for a few minutes. Add the coconut milk and stir gently until the sauce thickens. Pour over the fish and bake in the oven for 10-15 minutes at a medium heat. Serve with coconut rice.

## Fried fish fillets (Samaki wa kukaanga)

Serves 4 people

**Ingredients**

4 fish fillets

1 tsp garlic paste

1/2 tsp black pepper

1/2 tsp salt

juice of 1 lemon

2 oz fine white breadcrumbs

2 eggs

oil for frying

chopped coriander to garnish

**Method**

Marinade the fish fillets in the garlic, salt, pepper and lemon juice for 1 to 2 hours. Spread the breadcrumbs on the fillets and lastly dip the fish fillets into the beaten egg and fry until crisp and golden. Serve with a wedge of lemon and garnish with chopped coriander.

**Left:** Fish masala

## Barbecued prawns (Kamba wa kuchoma)

Serves 6 people

**Ingredients**

2 lbs medium prawns

1 tsp garlic paste

1/2 tsp red chilli powder

2 tbsps oil

2 green peppers cubed

2 onions cubed

juice of 2 lemons

lemon slices togarnish

salt and pepper to taste

**Method**

Mix all the ingredients in a large bowl and marinade prawns for 2-3 hours. Thread (on the skewers) alternate pieces of onion, prawn, green pepper and barbecue on a charcoal fire or grill in the oven basting the prawns with oil. Garnish with lemon slices. Serve immediately with a green salad.

## Prawns in coconut (Kamba wa kupaka)

Serves 6 people

**Ingredients**

1lb prawns shelled and cleaned

2 cups coconut milk

2 large tomatoes peeled and chopped

2 medium onions chopped

2-3 green chillies chopped

2 tbsps vegetable oil

1 tsp chilli powder or to taste

1 tsp garam masala

1/4 tsp ground turmeric

salt to taste

chopped coriander to garnish

**Method**

Fry the chopped onions in the oil for 5 minutes. Add the chopped tomatoes and green chillies and cook until the sauce thickens. Add salt, all the remaining spices and the prawns and blend them with half of the coconut milk and simmer until well cooked. Add the remaining coconut milk and cook for another 5minutes.

Sprinkle with the lemon juice and garnish with chopped coriander. Serve with rice or chapatis.

## Garlic prawns (Kamba wa vitunguuthomu)

Serves 6-8 people

**Ingredients**

2 lbs medium prawns peeled

1 tsp garlic paste

1 tsp ginger paste

1 tsp black pepper

1/2 cup cornflour

3 small eggs

2 onions finely chopped

1 green chilli finely chopped

1/2 tsp garlic paste, extra

2 tbsps tomato sauce

1 tbsp vinegar

1 tsp sugar

salt to taste

oil for frying

pinch of mace

chopped spring onions and coriander to garnish

**Method**

Marinade the prawns in the garlic, ginger, pepper and salt for an hour. Beat the eggs and add the cornflour, a pinch of salt and pepper and make a smooth batter. Dip the prawns in the batter then deep fry and put aside. Saute the chopped onion in 2 tbsps of oil. Add 1/2 tsp of garlic and the green chilli and cook for 2 minutes. Add the tomato sauce, vinegar and sugar, mix well and adjust the seasoning. Add the fried prawns and also add a few drops of water if necessary and allow to simmer for 5 minutes. Garnish with mace, spring onions and coriander. Serve with rice.

**Left:** Barbecued prawns

## Zanzibar lobster (Zanzibari kamba)

Serves 2 people

**Ingredients**

1 medium lobster

1 carrot grated

1/2 green pepper thinly sliced

1 tsp garlic paste

margarine or butter

grated cheese

salt and pepper to taste

1 cup white sauce

### white sauce

**Ingredients**

2 oz butter or margarine

2 cups warm milk

2 oz plain flour

1 cup water

salt and pepper

**Method**

Melt the butter or margerine in a small saucepan. Stir in the flour and cook over a low heat stirring with a wooden spoon. Gradually add the milk, water, salt and pepper, stirring constantly to keep the sauce smooth until the thickens. keep aside.

**Method**

Boil the lobster until soft. Remove the meat from the shell. Saute the carrot and green pepper in the butter until soft. Add the garlic paste, salt and pepper and cook for 2 minutes. Add the white sauce and cook for a further 2 minutes. Replace the meat in the shell and cover with the sauce. Sprikle with the grated cheese and put in a hot oven for a few minutes until it is brown.

## Prawns masala (kamba wa salo)

Serves 6 people

**Ingredients**

2 lbs prawns shelled and cleaned

2 medium onions chopped

6 medium tomatoes peeled and chopped

3 green chillies finely chopped

1 tsp garlic paste

1 tsp ginger paste

1 tsp garam masala

1 tsp ground cumin

1/2 tsp ground turmeric

4 tbsps vegetable oil

juice of 2 small lemons

salt and pepper to taste

chopped coriander to gsrnish

**Method**

Heat the oil and fry the onions until brown. Add the chopped tomatoes, lemon juice, and all the spices and cook for five minutes stirring frequently. Add the prawns and cook for 10-15 minutes. Add a little water if necessary and cook for a further 5 minutes and garnish with chopped coriander. Serve with chapatis or rice.

## Crab in coconut ( Kaa wa nazi)

Serves 6 people

**Ingredients**

10 medium sized crabs

1 onion chopped

1 tomato chopped

1 cup coconut milk

1 tsp garlic paste

salt and pepper to taste

**Method**

Wash the crabs throughly and boil for 10 to 15 minutes until tender. Remove the meat when cool. Saute the onion and tomato until soft. Add coconut milk and the crab meat and season it with salt and pepper and cook for further 5 to 10 minutes. Serve with rice or ugali.

**Left:** Zanzibar lobster

# Chicken & Meat dishes

## Chicken in coconut sauce (Kuku wa kupaka)

Serves 6-8 people

**Ingredients**

3 lb chicken cut into 8-10 pieces

1 onion finely chopped

2 medium tomatoes chopped

2 tsps garlic paste

1 tsp green chillies crushed

2 fresh green chillies

1/2 tsp turmeric

1 tbsp oil

2 cups coconut milk

juice of 1 lemon

salt to taste

coriander chopped to garnish

salt to taste

**Method**

Marinade the chicken pieces in garlic, chillies, turmeric, lemon juice and salt and leave for 2 - 3 hours. Saute the finely chopped onion in the oil and add the chopped tomatoes and mix thoroughly on a medium heat. Add two fresh green chillies and the coconut milk and stir all the time to make a thick gravy on a low heat. Keep aside. Roast the chicken pieces on charcoal or in an oven for 10 - 15 minutes until cooked. Place the chicken pieces in a dish and pour the thick coconut sauce over the roasted chicken and put the dish in the oven for 10 minutes, basting the chicken with the gravy from time to time. Garnish with chopped coriander and serve with coconut rice, sesame bread, mandazi, or mkate wa kumimina.

## Tandoori chicken (Kuku wa kuoka)

Serves 6 people

**Ingredients**

6 pcs skinned chicken joints or

1 chicken (3 lbs skinned and cut into small pieces)

1 small carton natural yogurt

1 tsp red chilli powder

1 tsp garam masala

1 tsp ground coriander

1 tsp ground cumin

1 tsp garlic paste

1 tsp ginger paste

2 fresh green chillies chopped

1 tbsp tomato puree

2 tbsps oil

a few drops of red food colouring

salt and pepper to taste

chopped coriander to garnish

**Method**

Marinade the chicken with all the ingredients for 4 hours or overnight. Either bake, or grill or barbecue the chicken on both sides. Garnish with chopped coriander. Serve on a bed of salad.

## Meat and vegetable stew (Mchuzi wa nyama na mboga)

Serves 6 people

**Ingredients**

1 lb meat cut into small pieces (goat or lamb)

2 medium tomatoes chopped

2 tsps tomato paste

2 onions chopped

1/2 tsp garlic paste

1/2 tsp ginger paste

2 tbsps oil

1 tbsp plain flour or some raw grated papaya

1 tsp curry powder or garam masala

2 medium potatoes cubed

2 carrots sliced

1  small cabbage chopped

1 cup peas

pinch of ground turmeric

salt, pepper and chilli to taste

chopped coriander to garnish

**Left:** Chicken in coconut sauce, Sesame bread and Coconut rice

**Method**

Heat the oil and fry the chopped onions lightly. Add the plain flour and saute for 2 minutes. Add the chopped tomatoes, turmeric, tomato puree, garlic, ginger, salt and pepper and saute for 2 to 3 minutes. Add the meat and saute for a further 2 to 3 minutes. Add sufficient hot water and cook for 45 minutes until the meat is tender. Add more water if necessary and cook for a further few minutes. Add all the vegetables and cook until the meat and vegetables are tender. Garnish with chopped coriander and serve with ugali or rice.

## Barbecued meat (Mishikaki)

Serves 6 people

Barbecued meat is sold by many street vendors in Zanzibar. Small pieces of beef are skewered then cooked over glowing charcoal, brushed with a chilli sauce to add flavour.

**Ingredients**

2 1/2 lbs lamb, rump or fillet steak cut into small pieces
1 tbsp red chilli powder
1/2 tsp black pepper
1 tbsp ginger paste
1 tbsp garlic paste
1 tbsp tomato paste (optional)
2 tbsps cooking oil
salt to taste
1 tbsp crushed raw papaya (an optional tenderiser for meat)

**Method**

Mix all the ingredients in a large bowl and marinade the meat overnight or for at least four hours in a refrigerator. Prepare a charcoal fire and grill the meat on skewers. Occasionally baste the meat with oil and also brush with a chilli sauce. Serve immediately with a green salad and Zanzibari sauce.

## Meat with banana puree (Mtori)

Serves 6 people

This dish is prepared with savoury bananas and is deliciously creamy.

**Ingredients**

1 lb stewing meat
6 small green bananas
2 onions chopped
2 tbsps butter
1 tsp garlic paste
1 tsp ginger paste
2 fresh green chillies
1/2 cup thick coconut milk
salt and pepper to taste

**Method**

Cut the meat into small pieces and marinade in the garlic, ginger and green chillies for one to two hours. Cook the meat in some water until tender. Peel the bananas and add to the meat with the chopped onions. Add water if necessary and allow to simmer until tender. Add the butter and mash the banana. Lastly add the thick coconut milk and cook over a low heat for a further 5 minutes.

## Meat curry (Mchuzi wa nyama)

Serves 6-8 people

Perfect with rice. You can substitute chicken as well.

**Ingredients**

1 1/2 lbs lamb cut into small pieces
2 large onions chopped
4 fresh tomatoes chopped or 1 tin chopped tomatoes
2 tbsps tomato puree
1 tsp garlic paste
1 tsp ginger paste
6 tbsps oil
2 tsps ground coriander
2 tsps ground cumin
1/2 tsp ground turmeric
1/2 tsp red chilli powder
1 tsp garam masala
4 tbsps natural yogurt
salt to taste
chopped coriander to garnish

**Left:** Mshikaki with sesame bread and salad and Zazibari sauce

**Whole dry spices**

2 sticks cinnamon

4 cardamom pods

4 cloves

1 tsp whole black peppercorns

1 tsp whole cumin seeds

2 fresh green chillies (slit)

**Method**

Heat the oil in a saucepan and fry the chopped onion until golden brown. Add all the whole dry spices and fry for 2 minutes. Add the tomatoes, puree and the remaining spices and cook over a low heat. Add the meat and cook over a medium heat stirring occasionally. Add 2 cups of warm water and cook until the meat is tender. Add the yogurt and cook for a further 2 minutes. Garnish with chopped coriander and serve hot with rice or chapatis.

## Lentil bhajia (Bhajia za dengu)

Serves 6 people

**Ingredients**

1 lbs green lentils skinned and cleaned (green moong daal)

1 large onion chopped

5-6 spring onions chopped

4-5 green chillies chopped

a small bunch of coriander chopped

1 tsp garlic paste

salt to taste

oil for frying

**Method**

Saok the lentils overnight or for at least 3 hours. Drain, rinse and grind to a rough puree in a food processor. Do not blend into a fine paste. Add all the chopped ingredients with salt to taste and mix well with a wooden spoon. Separate into small balls and deep fry the mixture for 3-4 minutes. Drain on kitchen paper and serve hot with coconut chutney or Zanzibari sauce.

## Yam and meat stew (Viyazi vikuu vya nyama)

Serves 6 people

**Ingredients**

2 medium yams

1 lb meat cut into small pieces (goat or lamb)

2 small onions chopped

3 tomatoes chopped

2 tbsps oil

2 stalks coriander chopped

2 cups of water or stock

salt to taste

**Method**

Peel and dice the yam and keep aside in salted water. heat the oil and fry the chopped onions lightly. Add the tomatoes, coriander, meat, salt and pepper and boil in two cups of water until the meat is tender. drain the yam and add to the meat stew and cook for 5-10 minutes. Serve hot with rice or ugali.

## Green bananas with beef or fish (Ndizi mbichi ya nyama au samaki)

Serves 6 people

"Bichi" means unripe and this is savoury banana dish which is popular in Zanzibar. You can also add cooked meat or fried minced meat if desired.

**Ingredients**

2 lbs green bananas (matoke) peeled and cubed

1 lb meat or fish

1 tbsps oil

2 onions chopped

2 tomatoes chopped

2-3 green chillies

1/2 tsp turmeric

1 cup thick coconut milk

lemon juice to taste

salt and pepper to taste

**Method**

Peel and slice the bananas and leave in salted water. Heat the oil in a saucepan and fry the chopped onion until soft. Add the chopped tomatoes, turmeric, salt, pepper and chillies and cook for 1 minute. Add meat or fish and one cup of hot water and simmer until the meat or fish is cooked. Add the drained bananas and cook for 10 minutes. Add the coconut milk, lemon juice and cook over a medium heat until the sauce thickens. Serve with rice or ugali.

---

**Left:** Lentil bhajia and Coconut chutney

# Vegetarian dishes

## Cassava in coconut  (Muhogo wa nazi)

Serves 6 people

A superb starter and a favourite in Zanzibar. You can also add fish boiled meat if desired.

### Ingredients

1 lb cassava (muhogo) Or 1 pkt frozen sliced cassava

2-3 green chillies

1 1/2 cups thick coconut milk

lemon juice to taste

salt to taste

### Method

Peel the cassava and cut into small slices about 2" thick, then boil in salted water until tender and drain. Put the coconut milk and whole green chillies in a saucepan and cook for 10 minutes until the sauce thickens. Add the cassava pieces and cook over a medium heat for 5-10 minutes. Add lemon juice and salt to taste and serve warm.

## Bread fruit in coconut (Sheli sheli wa nazi)

Same method as above

## Mixed vegetable curry (Mchuzi wa mboga mboga)

Serves 6 people

### Ingredients

*[handwritten: 3 carrots (diced) #2 potatoes, sliced thin small cauliflower head, florets]*

1 lb mixed vegetables cut to desired size (potatoes, peas, carrots, cabbage etc)

2-3  fresh tomatoes chopped *(1 small can diced)*

2 small onions ~~chopped~~ *diced [1 large]*

1 tsp garlic paste *(2 cloves)*

1 tsp tomato puree *(ketchup)*

~~1 tsp ground coriander~~

~~1 tsp ground cumin~~

1/4 tsp ground turmeric *— try ginger*

1/2 tsp mustard seeds *( )*

1/2 tsp cumin seeds *( )*

6 curry leaves *(curry powder) 1 tsp*

~~1~~ **2** fresh green chillies (slit) ~~or red chilli powder to taste~~ *jalap...o*

2 tbsps oil *olive*

salt to taste *(~ 1 1/2 tsp sea salt)*

*[handwritten: 2 Tbsp butter  1/4 cup milk]*

chopped coriander to garnish

### Method

Heat the oil and fry the chopped onions lightly until brown. Add the mustard seeds, cumin seeds, curry leaves and green chillies and cook for 2 minutes. Add the tomatoes and all the remaining ingredients and fry for a further 5 minutes mixing well. Cook on a low heat until the vegetables are tender. *covered* Add a ~~little water if~~ needed and cook for **15** minutes. Garnish with chopped coriander. Serve with rice or chapatis.

*[handwritten right margin: Add carrots, then potatoes, then cauliflower.  3/4 cup  → butter milk]*

## Cassava leaf stew (Mboga ya kisamvu)

Serves 6 people

This has an unexpected combination of flavours.

### Ingredients

2 cups cassava leaves (spinach can be use as a substitute)

1/2 cup finely chopped peanuts Or  1/2 cup  coconut milk

2 medium onions chopped

1 tbsp vegetable oil

salt to taste

### Method

Boil the kisamvu / spinach in salted water until soft. Saute the onions in oil, then add the finely chopped peanuts or coconut milk. Add the boiled kisamvu and cook for another 10 minutes. Serve with rice or ugali.

## Lentils in coconut (Mchuzi wa choroko)

Serves 6 people

### Ingredients

1 cup any type of lentils

1 medium onion chopped

1 medium tomato chopped

1/2 tsp garlic paste

1/2 tsp ground turmeric

**Left:** Cassava in coconut

1/2 tsp cumin seeds

1 green chilli

3 tbsps oil or margarine

1 cup coconut milk

juice of 1 lemon — 1 Tbsp

salt to taste

chopped coriander to garnish

### Method

Clean and wash the lentils thoroughly in cold water and soak for 1 hour. Saute the chopped onion in oil or margarine until soft. Add the lentils to 2 pints of water and bring to the boil. Remove any surface scum from lentils. Add the turmeric, chopped tomatoes, and chilli and simmer on a low heat for 1 hour partly covering the pan until the lentils are tender, stirring occasionally to prevent sticking. Add the salt and coconut milk and mix well. Heat the oil in a small frying pan over a medium heat and add the cumin seeds and garlic and fry until lightly browned. Add to the lentils with the lemon juice and stir well. Garnish with chopped coriander. Serve with chapatis or rice.

### Spinach with coconut and peanuts (Mchicha wa nazi na karanga)

Serves 6 people

### Ingredients

1 lb spinach

1 cup coconut milk

1/2 cup finely crushed roasted peanuts

2 medium onions chopped

2 medium tomatoes chopped

2 fresh green chillies

1 tbsp vegetable oil

salt to taste

### Method

Wash the spinach thoroughly in salted water then chop very finely and drain. Saute the chopped onions in vegetable oil until soft and add the spinach and cook for 3-5 minutes. Add the tomatoes, green chillies, chopped peanuts and coconut milk and cook for a further 10-15 minutes until tender. Serve hot with rice, chapatis or ugali.

### Aubergine and potato curry (Mchuzi wa biringani na viazi)

Serves 6 people

A simple but delicious curry.

### Ingredients

1 lb aubergines (~1)

1 lb potatoes (~3)

2 medium onions chopped (~1)

4 tbsps oil

2 tsp garam masala

1 tbsp tomato puree (1½ cup)

6 curry leaves (1 tsp curry powder)

juice of 1 lemon

salt to taste (2 tsp)

chopped coriander to garnish

+ 2 Tbsp butter at end

### Method

Cut the aubergine and potatoes into cubes. Heat the oil in a pan and fry the chopped onions. Add the vegetables curry leaves and fry for 10 minutes. Stir in the garam masala, tomato puree, salt and cook for 5 minutes. Add water if necessary and simmer for 10 minutes stirring occasionally. Add lemon juice and garnish with coriander. Serve hot with chapatis or rice.

### Cassava and beans (Mchanyato)

Serves 6- 8 people

### Ingredients

1/2 lb cassava

1 cup beans (red kidney beans)

1 cup coconut milk

1 onion chopped

salt and pepper to taste

### Method

Soak the beans overnight. Boil them in plenty of water for at least one hour and put to one side. Peel the cassava and cut into thin slices then boil in salted water. Saute the chopped onion until soft. Add the beans, coconut milk and cassava and cook for 20 to 30 minutes. When ready the consistency should be thick and runny - but not watery. Serve hot with ugali.

**Left:** Spinach with coconut and peanuts served with chapatis

## Pigeon peas in coconut (Mbaazi za nazi)

Serves 6 people

Often eaten for breakfast with mandazi (coconut doughnuts).

**Ingredients**

1 lb pigeon peas

2 small onions chopped

2-3 green chillies

1 cup thick coconut milk

1 tbsp oil

pinch of ground turmeric

juice of 1 lemon

coriander to garnish

salt to taste

**Method**

Boil the pigeon peas until tender and drain. Heat the oil and fry the chopped onions lightly. Add the chillies, turmeric and salt to taste and cook for 2 minutes. Add the pigeon peas and fry well. Add the coconut milk and cook until the sauce thickens. Lastly sprinkle with lemon juice and garnish with chopped coriander. Serve with mandazi, chapatis, rice or ugali.

## Bitter tomatoes (Nyanya mshumaa)

Serves 4 people

**Ingredients**

4 oz nyanya mshumaa

1 onion chopped

1 tomato chopped

1 cup coconut milk

pinch of ground turmeric

1 tsp oil

salt to taste

**Method**

Saute the onion in the oil until soft and add the chopped tomato and saute for another minute. Add the nyanya mshumaa, turmeric powder and salt to taste and cook for 5 minutes. Add the coconut milk and simmer until tender. Serve with chapatis, rice or ugali.

## Spicy lady's fingers (Bamiya la viungo)

Lady's fingers are vegetables native to Africa and are now grow in most countries around the world.

Serves 4 people

**Ingredients**

1 lb lady's fingers

2 medium onions chopped

2 tomatoes chopped

1/2 tsp chilli powder

2 stalks coriander chopped to garnish

salt and pepper to taste

**Method**

Wash the lady's fingers and dry completely. Cut off the tops and tips and slit each lady's finger lengthways. Mix the spices and marinade the lady's fingers for at least one hour. Heat the oil and fry the chopped onions lightly. Add the tomatoes and lady's fingers and cook for a further 10 to 15 minutes. Garnish with the chopped coriander. Serve with chapatis, rice or ugali.

## Roast sweet potatoes (Viazi vitamu vya kuchoma)

Serve 4 people

**Ingredients**

1 lb sweet potatoes

1/2 cup fat or margarine

**Method**

Wash and boil the sweet potatoes until half cooked and drain. Slice lengthways and brush with melted fat and grill until golden brown on both sides. Serve hot with stew or on their own as a snack.

**Left:** Pigeon peas in coconut served with mandazi

## Beans in coconut (Maharagwe)

This is a typical Swahili dish and is often eaten for breakfast

Serves 4-6 people

**Ingredients**

1 lb kidney beans

2 small onions chopped

2-3 green chillies

1 cup thick coconut milk

1 tbsp oil

pinch of ground turmeric

salt and pepper to taste

**Method**

Boil the beans until tender and drain. Heat the oil and fry the chopped onions lightly. Add the chillies, turmeric, salt and pepper and cook for 2 minutes. Add the beans and fry well. Add the coconut milk and cook until the sauce thickens.

Serve with rice, mandazi, chapatis or ugali.

## Roasted Bananas (Ndizi za kuchoma)

Serves 4 people

**Ingredients**

8 roasting bananas

butter or margarine

salt to taste

**Method**

Peel the bananas and roast on a charcoal brazier or cook under the grill until soft and brown on both sides. Slice lengthways and spread with a little fat and salt to taste. Serve hot as a snack or eat with vegetable and meat stew.

## Aubergine in coconut (Biringani wa nazi)

Serves 4 people

**Ingredients**

1 lb aubergine

1 onion chopped

1 tsp garlic paste

1 tsp turmeric

2 fresh chillies

1 tbsp oil

1/2 cup coconut milk

juice of 1 lemon

salt and pepper to taste

**Method**

Slice the aubergine and marinade in lemon juice. Heat the oil and fry the onions until soft. Add the garlic, turmeric, chillies, salt, pepper and aubergine and cook for a few minutes. Add the coconut milk and cook gently until the aubergine is tender and the coconut milk thickens. Serve hot with chapatis, rice or ugali.

**Left:** Maharagwe in coconut served with stiff porridge

# Sensational Savouries

## Corn on the cob in coconut (Mahindi ya nazi)

Serves 6-8 people

**Ingredients**

4 corn on the cob

1 cup coconut milk

2 medium tomatoes chopped

2 green chillies chopped

pinch of ground turmeric

juice of 1 lemon

salt to taste

chopped coriander to garnish

**Method**

Boil the corn in salted water until tender. Cut into 2 to 3 inch pieces (rings) and put to one side.

**Coconut sauce**

Take 1/2 cup of water, add the chopped tomatoes, salt, chilli, a pinch of turmeric, the lemon juice and bring to the boil. Add the coconut milk and stir constantly until the sauce bubbles then cook on a medium heat for 10 minutes. Add the pieces of corn and cook for a further 10 minutes on a low heat. Garnish with chopped coriander.

## Savoury potato balls (Bhajia ya batata)

Serves 6 people

**Ingredients**

4 boiled potatoes

1 tsp turmeric powder

1 tsp red chilli powder or to your taste

fresh coriander chopped

juice of 1 small lemon

a pinch of sugar

salt to taste

oil for frying

**Ingredients for batter**

2 tbsps gram flour

salt to taste

water to make a thick paste

**Method to make the batter**

Mix the flour, salt and water and make a thick paste. Put on one side.

**Method**

Peel and mash the potatoes. Add all the above spices and lemon juice to the potatoes and mix well. Make small balls from the mixture. Dip the balls in the batter and deep fry in oil until golden brown. Serve hot with tamarind sauce or coconut chutney.

## Meat kebabs (Kababu ya nyama)

Serves 6 people

A delicious starter.

**Ingredients**

1 lb minced meat

4 large eggs

3 slices white bread without crusts

1 tsp ginger paste

1 tsp garlic paste

1 tsp garam masala

1 cup breadcrumbs

1 medium onion finely chopped

4 green chillies finely chopped

4 stalks coriander chopped

salt and pepper to taste

oil for frying

**Method**

Soak the bread in water for a few minutes. Squeeze out all the water then mix the bread, minced meat, one egg and all the spices thoroughly. Divide the mixture into 18-20 equal portions and roll each between the palms into round or oblong shapes. Roll the kebabs in the breadcrumbs. Beat the remaining eggs then dip the kebabs in the beaten eggs and deep fry over a medium heat, turning once or twice until golden brown. Drain on kitchen paper. Serve them hot on a bed of green salad and with a chutney of your choice.

**Left:** Corn on the cob in coconut

## Chicken shashlik kebabs (Mishikaki wa kuku)

Serves 6-8 people

**Ingredients**

1 lb boneless chicken cut into small cubes

1 tsp garlic paste

1 tsp ginger paste

1 tsp yogurt

1 tbsp tomato puree

2 medium onions

2 large green peppers

2-3 eggs

salt and pepper to taste

oil for frying

cocktail sticks /skewers

**Method**

Cut the green pepper and onions into small square pieces and put them to one side. Mix all the ingredients, except the eggs, and marinade the chicken cubes for at least one hour. Thread alternate pieces of onion, chicken, pepper, chicken, onion or the other way round on to cocktail sticks. Lastly coat the chicken-threaded cocktail stick with breadcrumbs, dip into the whisked egg and deep fry over a medium heat on both sides until golden brown. Drain on kitchen paper and serve with salad as a side dish.

## Potato patties (Mbatata patties)

Serves 4 people

These can be eaten as a delicious snack any time of the day. They are to be found at many street stalls in Zanzibar.

**Ingredients**

1 lb potatoes

2 beaten eggs

1 cup breadcrumbs

salt and pepper to taste

oil for frying

**Stuffing**

1/2 lb minced meat

2 onions very finely chopped

2 green chillies chopped

1 tsp ginger paste

1 tsp garlic paste

1/4 tsp ground turmeric

1 tsp garam masala

some mint and coriander chopped

**Method**

Boil the potatoes and mash them very finely and add salt and pepper to taste.

**Stuffing**

Mix the minced meat with garlic, ginger and salt and fry stirring continuously until the minced meat is cooked. Let it cool then add all the spices, chopped onions, mint and coriander. Divide the mashed potato into 8 parts. Take one part of the mashed potato, flatten it between your palms and put one tablespoon of stuffing in the centre. Then fold the mashed potato over the stuffing so it is all well covered. Cover the potato patty with breadcrumbs and do the same with the remaining mixture. Now dip each potato patty into the beaten egg and deep fry on both sides over a medium heat. Serve them hot on a bed of green salad with a chutney of your choice.

## Spicy potatoes (Mbatata ya pilipili)

Serves 4-6 people

An easy and very popular dish

**Ingredients**

1 lb potatoes

1/2 tsp garlic paste

1/2 tsp turmeric

1/2 tsp chilli powder

1 tsp ground cumin

1 tsp ground coriander

2 tbsps tomato puree

2 tbsps oil

lemon juice to taste

pinch of sugar

salt to taste

coriander to garnish

**Left:** Chicken shashlik

**Method**

Boil the potatoes, drain and skin them, then cut into small pieces. Heat the oil in a saucepan and add all the spices and tomato puree and let the mixture sizzle for 5 minutes. Add the potatoes and mix well. Add 1/4 cup of hot water if necessary. Lastly add a pinch of sugar and the lemon juice and garnish with freshly chopped coriander. Serve hot with rice, chapatis or as a side dish.

## Zanzibar pizza (Khima mani)

Serves 6 people

**Ingredients**

2 cups plain flour

1/2 tsp salt

1/2 cup water

1 cup oil

1 lb finely minced meat

1 tsp garlic paste

1 tsp ginger paste

3 - 4 fresh chillies chopped

1 onion very finely chopped

3 stalks fresh coriander chopped

6 eggs

salt and pepper to taste

**Method**

Sieve the flour into a bowl, add salt and enough water to make a smooth dough and knead for 2 - 3 minutes. Divide the dough into 6 equal balls and put in a shallow dish. Pour the oil over them, making sure they are well coated. Then cover and put on one side for 2 hours.

**Stuffing**

Mix the minced meat with the salt, pepper, garlic and ginger paste and fry, stirring continuously until the meat is cooked. Allow to cool. Add the finely chopped onion, coriander and chopped green chillies to the prepared meat and keep aside. Stretch the dough balls into a very thin 10 inch circle on a chopping board or metal tray. Make sure the edges are thinner than the centre. Put 2 tablespoons of the prepared meat mixture in the centre of the circle. Break an egg on top of the meat and close the circle by bringing 2 sides up over the other 2 sides, folding it like a square envelope. Put one teaspoon of oil on a medium hot griddle, and bake this envelope over a low heat on both sides until the egg is cooked. Repeat this process with the remaining dough. Cut into four squares and serve with salad and tomato chutney.

## Mixed bhajia (Bhajia)

Serves 6 people

**Ingredients**

2 cups gram flour

2 medium potatoes peeled and sliced

2 medium onions cut into rings

1 aubergine cut into thin slices

a few whole fresh chillies

1 tsp chilli powder

1 tsp ground coriander

1 tsp ground cumin

chopped coriander

1/4 tsp bicarbonate of soda

salt to taste

**Method**

Mix the gram flour with 1/2 cup of water and make a smooth batter. Add the spices, chopped coriander and bicarbonate of soda and mix well. Heat the oil. Dip the sliced potatoes into the batter and deep fry on a medium heat. Do the same with the onion rings, aubergine slices and fresh chillies. Drain them on kitchen paper and serve hot with coconut or tamarind chutney.

**Left:** Zanzibar pizza

### Bean bhajia (Bhajia za kunde)

Serves 4 people

Bhajias are one of the most popular snacks which can be bought at stalls on the street in Zanzibar and there are many different varieties. They are usually eaten with different kinds of chutney.

**Ingredients**

1 lb beans

1 onion chopped

2-3 green chillies

salt

**Method**

Soak the beans overnight or for at least 3/4 hours. Drain, rinse and grind to a rough puree in a food processor with chillies and onion. Add a little water if necessary. Do not blend into a fine paste. Separate into small balls and deep fry the mixture for 3-4 minutes, Drain on kitchen paper and serve hot with coconut chutney, red chilli sauce and Zanzibari sauce.

### Zanzibari sauce (Rojo)

**Ingredients**

1 tbsp flour

2 cups water

1/4 tsp turmeric

1/4 tsp red chilli powder

1 small unripe mango or

juice of 1 lemon

salt

**Method**

Peel the mango and cut into small pieces and boil in very little water. When cool blend it and keep aside. Mix all the ingredients and boil, stirring continuously. Add mango pulp or lemon juice and cook for 1 minute. Serve with boiled potatoes, barbecued meat or on bhajias.

### Zanzibar mix

Serve with bean bhajia. Add small pieces of boiled potatoes, potato balls, very thin crispy potatoes or cassava chips, coconut chutney and Zanzibari sauce.

### Savoury spiced pancakes (Chila)

Serves 4 people

Chila can be sweet or savoury and are similar to pancakes.

**Ingredients**

2 cups gram flour

1 tsp chilli powder

1/4 tsp turmeric

a few stalks chopped coriander

salt to taste

oil for frying

**Method**

Mix the gram flour with 1/2 cup of water and make a smooth batter as for pancakes. Add all the spices and mix well. Heat a little oil in a pan and pour in enough batter for one pancake. Cook on both sides and serve warm with tamarind or coconut chutney.

### Roasted cassava (Muhogo wa kuchoma)

Roasted cassava is one of the most popular snacks which can be bought at stalls on the streets of Zanzibar.

**Method**

Wash cassava thoroughly. Peel and roast them on an open fire or under a grill. When ready, cut in half lengthwise and serve with salt and chilli powder.

### Sweet potatoes (Viazi tamu)

**Method**

Wash the sweet potatoes and roast them on an open fire or under a grill. When ready cut in half lengthwise and eat the soft inner part.

**Left:** Zanzibar mix

### Samosas (Sambusa)

These are delicious Indian snacks which are very common and popular in Zanzibar. There are many different varieties of fillings in these triangle shaped pastries. You can freeze them nd they can be fried straight from the freezer.

### Samosa pastry

You can also use ready-made samosa pastry available in Indian and Chinese shops.

### Ingredients

1 cup plain flour
1/2 tsp salt
1 cup water
1 cup oil

### Method

Sieve the flour into a bowl, add salt and enough water to make a soft dough and knead for 2-3 minutes. Divide the dough into four equal balls. using a chapati board or a flat surface, roll each ball evenly into a circle of about four inches in diameter. Spread each circle evenly with oil then sprinkle flour over the top of the oil. Place each circle on the first and repeat the oil and flour procedure. Gently roll out into a large circle of about 8-9 inches in diameter, making sure that the circles are turned upside down to keep all the same size while rolling. Using an iron griddle or a frying pan, very lightly fry each circle on both sides without using any oil. Leave to cool. Now cut the layers into 3 strips and peel off the pieces to make 12 samosa. Keep the strips under a damp tea towel.

### Meat samosas (sambusa ya nyama)

### Ingredients

1 lb minced meat - mutton or beef
2-3 large onions finely chopped
1/2 tsp ginger paste
1/2 tsp garlic paste
1/2 tsp ground cinnamon
1 tsp garam masala
2-3 green chillies finely chopped
4 stalks coriander finely chopped
salt and pepper to taste

### Method

Mix the minced meat with the salt, pepper, garlic and ginger paste and fry on a medium heat stirring continuously until the meat is cooked. Allow to cool. Mix the finely chopped onion, coriander, green chillies and all the spices with the prepared meat. keep aside to fill the samosa pastry. This will make 12 samosas.

### Fish samosas (Sambusa ya samaki)

### Ingredients

1 lb white fish
1 onion finely chopped
1 tsp garlic
1/2 tsp garam masala
2-3 green chillies finely chopped
4 stalks coriander chopped
juice of 1 lemon
salt and pepper to taste

### Method

Marinade the fish in garlic, lemon juice and salt. Cook the fish on a medium heat until it is cooked. Debone the fish and mix with all the remaining ingredients and process in a food processor. keep aside to fill the samosa pastry. This will make 12 samosas.

### Vegetable samosas (Sambusa ya mboga)

### Ingredients

1/2 lb potatoes boiled and cut into very small cubes
1/2 lb vegetables of your choice chopped
1/2 tsp garlic
1 tbsp oil
1 onion finely chopped
1 tsp garm masala
2-3 green chillies finely chopped
4 stalks coriander finely chopped
salt and pepper to taste

---

**Left:** Samosas

## Method

Mix the vegetables with the salt, pepper and garlic and cook on a medium heat with 1 tbsp oil for 5 minutes until the vegetables are soft. Allow to cool then add all the remaining ingredients and keep aside to fill the samosa pastry. This will make 12 samosas.

## Paste

With a few spoonfuls of plain flour and water prepare a thickish paste to seal the samosa pastry.

## To fill the samosas

take one strip and fold it together to form a cone and stuff with a tablespoon of prepared filling. Fold the flap over and around the pastry cone, binding with the above paste, so that a tight triangle is formed and no holes can be seen at any of the corners.

## Diagram

A B C D forms a cone

D E folds the flap

F folds and binds with paste.

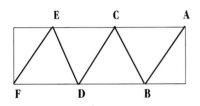

## Shish kebab (mshikaki wa nyama ya kusaga)

Serves 6 people

## Ingredients

1 lb minced meat

2 slices white bread without crusts

1 tsp ginger paste

1 tsp garlic paste

1 tsp garam masala

1 medium onion finely chopped

4 green chillies finely chopped

4 stalks coriander chopped

salt and pepper to taste

## Method

Soak the bread in water for a few minutes. Squeeze out all the water then mix the bread, minced meat, onion and all the spices throughly. Divide the mixture into 12 equal portions and roll each between the palms into oblong shapes and roll the kebabs on a thin rolling pin. Slide the kebab from the rolling pin and place one by one on a greased tray and bake or grill on a medium heat. Serve them hot on a bed of green salad and with a chutney of your choice.

**Left:** Shish kebab

# Sweet Snacks

### Rice bread (Mkate wa kumimina)

Serves 6 people

A favourite of Zanzibaris.

**Ingredients**

11/2 cups rice

1 sachet yeast

1/3 cup coconut milk

1/2 cup caster sugar

1 egg

1 tsp coarse cardamom powder

3 - 4 tbsps oil

**Method**

Soak the rice for 4 - 5 hours or overnight, then drain. Grind the rice with the coconut milk and sugar in a mixer until it is fine and creamy. Add the yeast and mix well. Cover and keep in a warm place for 1 - 2 hours until it has doubled in size. Lastly add one egg and the cardamom. If too thick add warm water. Leave for a further 5-10 minutes. Put 1 tbsp of oil in a baking dish and put on the cooker. Lower the heat and pour in 1/2 the mixture and cook for 5 minutes over a very low heat. Grill or transfer the dish to a preheated oven, cover and bake for 15 minutes in a medium hot oven. Serve warm with tea or kuku wa kupaka.

### Rice cakes (Vitumbua)

Serves 6-8 people

This is a variation on the theme of rice bread and these rice cakes are delicious for breakfast.

**Ingredients**

2 cups rice

1 sachet yeast

1 cup coconut milk

1 egg

1 tbsp crushed cardamom

1 cup sugar

oil for frying

**Method**

Soak the rice for 2 - 3 hours or overnight, then drain. Grind the rice with the coconut milk and sugar until it is fine and creamy. Add the yeast and cardamom and mix well. Keep in a warm place for 1 - 2 hours until it has doubled. Lastly add one egg. If too thick add warm milk and leave for a further 5 minutes. Warm a special vitumbua karai with one tablespoon of oil and pour a ladleful of the mixture and cook for 5 minutes over a medium heat. When firm turn the other side to cook. Serve warm with tea.

### Coconut doughnuts (Mandazi)

Serves 4 people

These are one of the most common and popular foods in Zanzibar. Try them for breakfast.

**Ingredients**

2 cups plain flour

5 tbsps sugar

1 cup coconut milk

1 tsp coarsely ground cardamom

1 sachet yeast

oil for frying

**Method**

Mix all the ingredients with the coconut milk and bind into a dough. Leave this dough in a warm place for 4-5 hours to rise. Then knead the dough well and roll out until 1/2 inch thick. Cut into triangles or required shapes and leave for a further 15 minutes. Deep fry each mandazi in hot oil over a medium heat on both sides to a deep tan colour. Drain on kitchen paper to remove excess oil. Serve with tea or mbaazi.

### Egg Sweet/Mahsub (Kashata ya mayai)

Serves 6-8 people

This is a kind of confectionery, typically eaten in Indian house in Zanzibar.

**Ingredients**

1 cup eggs (4-5 eggs)

1 cup sugar

---

**Left:** Vitumbua, Mandazi and Mkate wa kumimina

1 cup soft margarine, butter or ghee

1 tbsp gram flour

1 tsp coarsely ground cardamom

finely chopped almonds and pistachios to garnish

**Method**

Mix the eggs, sugar, margarine, gram flour and cardamom thoroughly. In a heavy bottomed saucepan cook the mixture over a medium heat stirring constantly until lightly golden. Pour the mixture into a greased square tray. Sprinkle with nuts and gently press flat. Cut into squares while warm.

## Soft doughnuts (Kaimati)

Serves 6-8 people

Children will love them and the rose water flavoured syrup is an interesting twist.

**Ingredients**

1 cup plain flour

2 tsps rice flour

3/4 cup water

1 sachet yeast

1 tsp cardamom powder

2 tbsps coconut milk

**Ingredients for syrup**

1 cup sugar

1 cup water

pinch of saffron

1/2 tsp ground cardamom / vanilla essence / rosewater

1/2 tsp lemon juice

**Method**

Mix all the syrup ingredients with the water and boil until a fairly thick syrup is formed. Put on one side. Mix the yeast with the plain flour, rice flour, coconut milk and cardamom and bind it into a soft batter with 1/2 a cup of water. Cover and set aside until it almost doubles. Heat the oil in a deep frying pan and drop a dessertspoon of the mixture into the hot oil and deep fry until golden brown. Drain well then dip into the syrup while still hot. Serve with tea.

## Peanut cake (Keki ya njugu)

Serve 4-6 people

Ingredients

2 1/2 cups peanuts

1/2 cup sugar

4 oz butter or margarine

2 cups self raising flour

1 tsp baking powder

3 eggs

1/2 cup milk

**Method**

Preheat the oven 15 minutes before the required time. Clean and crush the peanuts and keep aside. mix the sugar and margarine and mix thoroughly beating well. Add the beaten egg and mix, gradually adding a little flour with baking powder. Add milk and mix thoroughly. Put the mixture in a flat tin and smooth the top and bake until light brown. When cool, cut into any shape you prefer. Serve with tea as a snack.

## Rice Pancakes (Chila)

Serves 4 people

A favourite of Zanzibaris.

**Ingredients**

1 1/2 cups rice

1 sachet yeast

1 cup coconut milk

2 tbsps sugar or to taste

1 tsp coarse cardamom powder

3-4 tbsps oil

**Method**

Soak the rice for 2-3 hours or overnight, then drain. Grind the rice with the coconut milk and sugar in a mixer until it is fine and creamy. Add the yeast and cardamom and mix well. Cover and keep in a warm place for 1-2 hours until it has doubled in size. If too thick add warm water. Leave for a further 5-10 minutes. Put 1 tsp of oil in a non-stick frying pan or griddle and pour in 1/4 of the mixture and cook for 3 minutes over a very low heat on one side. Serve warm with tea.

**Left:** Soft doughnuts

# Rice dishes

Rice is a staple part of people's diet in Zanzibar. It is eaten with most meals.

## Meat pilau (Pilau ya nyama)

Serves 6 people

Zanzibar spices gives a delicious touch to this recipe. You can also substitute chicken or prawns.

### Ingredients

1 1/2 lb meat - goat or lamb

2 cups rice

2 cups water

2 medium onions chopped

1 tsp garlic paste

2 tsps garam masala

1 cup coconut milk (optional)

2 tbsps vegetable oil

1 chicken stock cube

1 oz cashew nuts

1 oz raisins

### Dry whole spices

3 cinnamon pieces

1 tsp black peppercorns

1 tsp cumin seeds

1 tsp cardamom pods

1/2 tsp cloves

salt to taste

### Method

Soak the rice in water for about 30 minutes, then drain. Saute the chopped onion. Add the whole spices, garlic paste, garam masala, cashew nuts and raisins and fry for 5 minutes. Add the chicken stock, the meat pieces and coconut milk and allow to simmer over a medium heat for 5 minutes. Add the drained rice and continue to cook for a few minutes. Add 3 cups of boiling water and cook for 10 minutes uncovered. Turn the heat down to low, cover the pot tightly and simmer for 15 minutes or put in an oven and cook for 15-20 minutes at a medium temperature. Serve with onion salad (kachumbari).

## Coconut rice (Wali wa nazi)

Serves 6-8 people

Coconut milk gives rice an exotic touch.

### Ingredients

2 cups basmati rice

3 cups thin coconut milk *(2 cups nazi milk + 1 cup water)*

~~1/2 cup thick coconut milk~~

salt to taste

### Method

Soak the rice in water for 20 minutes and drain. Put the rice, salt and 3 cups of thin coconut milk in a pan and bring to the boil. Reduce heat and simmer slowly until the rice is done. Add the thick coconut milk and simmer for a further 5 to 10 minutes or put in the oven. Serve hot with any meat or chicken dishes.

## Biriani (Biriani)

Serves 6-8 people

A dish which is often eaten at celebrations.

### Ingredients

1 medium sized chicken (skinned and cut into small pieces) Or

2 lbs meat cut into small pieces

3 cups basmati rice

1 cup oil

4-5 fresh tomatoes chopped or

1 tin chopped tomatoes

3 tbsps tomato puree

1/2 tsp strands of saffron

1 tbsp garlic paste

1 tbsp ginger paste

1 tbsp garam masala

1 tsp coriander

1 tsp chilli powder

2 cups natural yogurt

3-4 green chillies

1 1/2 lbs onions

3 potatoes (cut into 4 pcs)

coriander chopped

**Left:** Meat pilau and onion salad

**Dry whole spices**

1 tsp cardamom pods

1 tsp black peppercorns

3 cinnamon pieces

1/2 tsp cloves

1 tsp cumin seeds

**Method**

Wash the rice and let it soak for 20 minutes or more. Heat the oil and fry the chopped onions until golden brown and put on one side. Peel and cut the potatoes into 4 pieces and fry them until lightly brown and put on one side. Marinade the chicken or meat (whatever you are using). Mix together half the quantity of the dry whole spices, yogurt, tomatoes, tomato puree, garlic, ginger, salt, fried potatoes, fried onions, half the saffron and all the ground spices. Preheat the oven to gas mark 2, 300 degrees F (150 degrees C). Par boil the rice with the remaining dry whole spices in plenty of salted water, then drain and rinse it under cold running water. Put 2 tbsps of oil in a saucepan and add the marinated chicken or meat. Put the par boiled rice on top of the chicken or meat and add the saffron strands and mix lightly. Spread some oil on top of the rice and cover very tightly and put the saucepan in a preheated oven for 1 hour 30 minutes or longer. Serve hot with onion salad (kachumbari) or raita (Yogurt).

## Wheat and meat stew (Bokoboko)

Serves 6-8 people

Bokoboko is a typical Zanzibari dish made for special occasions. It is usually served when relatives return from Mecca after performing the Islamic pilgrimage or Haj.

**Ingredients**

2 lbs broken wheat

1 1/2 lb chicken or meat

4 tomatoes chopped

2 onions chopped

1 cup ghee or oil

2 tbsps grated ginger

1 tbsp ginger paste

4 fresh green chillies

1 tbsp black peppercorns

crisp fried onions

mixed spices

salt to taste

chopped mint or coriander to garnish

**Method**

Cover the wheat with water and soak overnight. Saute the chopped onions until they are soft. Add the chopped tomatoes, green chillies, ginger paste, salt and cook the chicken or meat with some water until tender. Put to one side. Melt one cup of ghee or oil in a large pot. Add the grated ginger, whole black pepper, salt, soaked wheat and cook with sufficient water. Continue boiling, stirring frequently, and adding water if necessary until the wheat is very soft. Now add the cooked meat and cook over a medium heat, stirring vigorously so the meat is mixed thoroughly and the mixture has the consistency of thick porridge. Serve very hot on a big platter. Garnish with hot ghee, crisply fried onions, mixed spices and chopped mint and coriander.

## Stiff porridge (Ugali)

Serves 4 people

Ugali is a staple food in Tanzania and also in many other African countries. Made of maize, millet or cassava flour, it is a substitute for bread and rice in the African diet. It is generally more popular in mainland Tanzania than in Zanzibar.

**Ingredients**

1 cup white maize meal

2 cups water

1 tbsp oil or butter

salt to taste

**Method**

Boil the water ina bottomed saucepan then add the salt and oil. Sprinkle maize meal into the boiling water and stir continuously until it thickens over a medium temperature. Serve with any stew or curry.

**Left:** Wheat and meat stew

## Prawn Pilau (Pilau ya kamba)

Serves 6 people

**Ingredients**

2 cups rice

2 cups water

2 lbs prawns shelled and cleaned

2 medium onions chopped

2 tomatoes chopped

1 tsp garlic paste

2 tsps garam masala

1/2 cup coconut milk

2 tbsps vegetable oil

1 green pepper cut into small pieces

2 green chillies

juice of one lemon

salt and pepper to taste

chopped spring onions and coriander to garnish

**Dry whole spices**

2 cinnamon pieces

1 tsp black peppercorns

1 tsp cumin seeds

1 cardamom pods

1/2 tsp cloves

1/2 tsp grated nutmeg

**Method**

Marinade the prawns in the garlic, lemon juice, salt and pepper for 30 minutes. Soak the rice in water for about 30 minutes, then drain. Saute the chopped onions until soft. Add tomatoes, green pepper and cook for 3 minutes. Add all the ingredients except the coconut milk, prawns, rice and water and saute for 5 minutes. Add the prawns and coconut milk and cook over the medium heat for another 5 minutes. Add the drained rice and continue to cook for a few minutes. Add 2 cups of boiling water and cook for 10 minutes uncovered. Turn the heat down to low, cover the pot tightly and simmer for 15 minutes or put in an oven and cook at a medium temperature. Garnish with chopped green onions and coriander. Serve with onion salad.

## Vegetable pilau (Pilau ya mboga)

Serves 6 people

**Ingredients**

2 cups rice

2 cups water

2 medium onions chopped

1 tsp garlic paste

2 tsps garam masala

1 cup coconut milk

2 tbsps vegetable oil

2 medium potatoes peeled and chopped into cubes

2 carrots peeled and sliced

1/2 lb peas

1 green pepper cut into small pieces

2 green chillies

salt to taste

**Dry whole spices**

3 cinnamon pieces

1 tsp black peppercorns

1 tsp cumin seeds

1 cardamom pods

1/2 tsp cloves

1/2 tsp grated nutmeg

**Method**

Soak the rice in water for about 30 minutes, then drain. Saute the chopped onions. Add all the ingredients except the coconut milk, rice and water, and allow to cook over a medium heat for 5 minutes. Add the drained rice and 2 cups of boiling water and cook for 10 minutes uncovered. Add the coconut milk and cook on a low heat stirring occasionally, add water if necessary. Cover tightly and put in an oven and cook for 15-20 minutes at a medium temperature. Serve with onion salad.

**Left:** Prawn pilau

# Desserts

Most Zanzibaris have a sweet tooth and these recipes offer an exciting combination of spices and coconut milk together with more typical pudding ingredients.

## Coconut sweet (Kashata ya nazi)

Serves 6-8 people

Very quick and easy to prepare and eaten as a snack.

**Ingredients**

1 cup milk

1 cup desiccated coconut

1/2 cup sugar

1/2 tin  condensed milk

1 tbsp cardamom crushed

**Method**

Boil 1 cup of milk with the sugar over  a medium heat. Add the desiccated coconut, condensed milk and cardamom and cook until the mixture thickens. It is possible to  tint the mixture to a pale green or pale pink colour with food colouring. Put into a greased  dish  and cut into diamond shapes. Store in an airtight container.

## Varango  halwa (Halua ya uwanga)

Serves 6-8 people

A sweet dish which is often served at a celebrations such as weddings.

**Ingredients**

1 cup edible starch (varango)

2 cups sugar

1 cup oil (ghee)

1/4 tsp nutmeg (optional)

1 tsp whole cardamom seeds

100 gms flaked blanched almonds

pinch of saffron

pinch of red or orange food colouring

**Method**

Take two cups of water and soak the starch overnight if possible or for  at least one hour. Sieve the mixture a few times in cold water. Put the mixture in a saucepan and add all the ingredients except the nuts and cook over a  high heat stirring continuously so the mixture does not stick to the pan or become thick and sticky. Reduce the heat and add half the nuts and mix well. Pre-heat the oven to 160 degrees C (gas Mark 3 or 325 F) and put the mixture into the oven for 10 to 15 minutes. Serve in a shallow dish and decorate with the remaining nuts. You can serve halwa warm  or cold with black coffee.

## Caramel Pudding (Pudding ya mayai)

Serves 6 people

**Ingredients**

1 pint milk

4 eggs

6 tbsps sugar

2 tsps vanilla essence

**Method**

Put 3 tbsps sugar in a small saucepan and cook over a low heat until the sugar has melted. Remove from the heat and immediately pour the melted sugar into an ovenproof dish and allow to cool. Beat together the eggs, milk, vanilla essence and 3 tbsps of sugar (or to your taste) in a large mixing bowl. Pour the whisked mixture into the cooled ovenproof dish and place in a preheated moderately hot oven for 40 minutes or until the caramel pudding is cooked.  Let it cool. Chill in the refrigerator for a few hours before turning out onto a serving dish.

## Avocado whip (Pudding ya peya)

Serves 4-6 people

A delicious, rich and creamy  dessert. In Zanzibar, avocados are known as 'butter pears' and people prefer to consider them a sweet, often just mashing them with sugar.

**Ingredients**

2 medium ripe avocado pears

1/2 tin condensed milk

crushed ice

**Left:** Coconut sweet

**Method**

Peel the avocados and remove the flesh. Put into a blender and blend with the milk until smooth. Chill in a refrigerator. Serve with crushed ice in a glass fruit bowl.

## Tropical fruit salad (Matunda salad)

Serves 6 people

An ideal salad for a summer's day, full of Zanzibar's exotic fruit.

**Ingredients**

1 small papaya

1/2 medium pineapple

1/2 medium watermelon

1 ripe mango

2 bananas

2 oranges

juice of 2 lemons

juice of 2 oranges

6/8 purple passion fruits

1/2 cup sugar or to your taste

pinch of salt

**Method**

Grate the rind for zest and squeeze the juice from the 2 lemons and 2 oranges. Mix the zest and juice and boil for 3 minutes with the sugar. Chill the syrup in the refrigerator. Cut all the fruit into cubes. Add the banana slices and passion fruit seeds and a pinch of salt. Pour the syrup over the fruit salad and chill in the refrigerator. Serve in a glass fruit bowl.

## Rice pudding (Firni)

Serves 6 people

**Ingredients**

1/2 cup of rice flour

5 cups milk

3/4 cup sugar

1/4 tsp saffron

1 tbsp crushed cardamom

2 tbsps shredded almonds

2 tbsps shredded pistachios

**Method**

Put the rice flour into a large pan. Add the milk and cook over a medium heat for about 20 minutes stirring continuously until creamy. Add the sugar, crushed cardamom and saffron and cook until the sugar dissolves. Serve in a glass bowl and garnish with almonds and pistachios. Serve chilled.

## Papaya in coconut (Papai la nazi)

Serves 6-8 people

**Ingredients**

1 lb papaya grated

1 cup coconut milk

1/2 cup sugar

1 tbsp crushed cardamom

**Method**

Boil the grated papaya in plenty of water until soft and drain, then put to one side. Take one cup of coconut milk, add sugar and cardamom and cook over a low heat. Add the papaya and mix well. If dry add some milk and put in the oven for 5 - 10 minutes. Garnish with crushed cardamom.

## White marrow milk shake (Mungunye shuruba)

Serves 4-6 people

**Ingredients**

1 lb white marrow

1 litre milk

sugar to taste

1 tsp ground cardamom

pinch of nutmeg

crushed almonds

**Method**

Skin and grate the marrow. Mix it with milk and place in a saucepan over a low heat until soft. Add sugar and cardamom and cook for another 5 minutes. Mash or blend the mixture lightly and garnish with almonds and nutmeg. Serve cold.

**Left:** Tropical fruit salad

### Fried vermicelli (Tambi za kukaanga)

Services 6-8 people

This is a favourite of Zanzibaris and is mostly eaten as the meal to break the fast during the month of Ramadhan (the fasting month).

**Ingredients**

4 oz vermicelli (thin)

1/2 cup sugar

3 tbsps vegetable oil

1/2 cup milk

1 tbsps crushed cardamom

1 pinch of saffron

2 tbsps crushed almonds

2 tbsps raisins or sultans

**Method**

Fry the dry vermicelli in oil over a low heat until golden brown. Add the sugar, cardamom, saffron, sultanas and milk and cook for 5 - 7 minutes. Separate it with a fork and put in the oven for 10 minutes until it is dry. Garnish with crushed almonds.

### Vermicelli in coconut  (Tambi za nazi)

Serves 6-8 people

**Ingredients**

4 oz vermicelli (medium)

1 cup coconut milk

1/2 cup sugar

1 tbsp crushed cardamom

**Method**

Boil the vermicelli in plenty of water until soft, and drain. Put one cup of coconut milk into a saucepan, add the sugar and cardamom and cook over a low heat. Add the vermicelli and mix well. If dry, add some milk and put in an oven for 5 - 10 minutes. Sprinkle with crushed cardamom.

### Rice flour dessert (Vipopo ya uwanga)

Serves 6-8 people

**Ingredients**

1/2 cup rice flour

1/2 cup plain flour

1/2 cup sugar

1 1/2 cups coconut milk or ordinary milk

1 tsp ground cardamom

1 cup water

**Method**

Boil one cup of water then add the flours and mix well to make a stiff dough. When it is cool make very small balls and put on one side. Put the coconut milk in a saucepan and cook over a medium heat with the sugar and cardamom. When the mixture boils, put in the balls and cook for 10 minutes over a low heat until the liquid is absorbed. Serve warm or cold.

### Sweet bananas in  coconut (Ndizi mbivu)

Serves 6 people

A typical Zanzibari pudding with a delicious exotic flavour.

**Ingredients**

6 large ripe plantain bananas

1/2 cup sugar

3 cups thin coconut milk

1 cup thick coconut milk

1 tsp crushed cardamom

**Method**

Peel the bananas, cut in half lengthwise and place in a frying pan. Mix the sugar and crushed cardamom into the thin coconut milk. Pour over the bananas and simmer very slowly until tender. Add the thick coconut milk and simmer for a further 10 minutes over a low heat. Serve warm or cold.

### Baked Bananas (Ndizi za kuoka)

Serves 6 people

**Ingredients**

8 small bananas

lemon juice

brown sugar

1/2 tsp cinnamon powder

a pinch of nutmeg

fresh cream

**Left:** Fried vermicelli and Vermicelli in coconut

**Method**

Peel the bananas and cut them in half lengthwise. Sprinkle with brown sugar, lemon juice and the cinnamon powder and bake in a pre-heated moderate oven for 20-30 minutes until they become soft. Garnish with nutmeg. Serve warm with fresh cream.

## Faludo dessert (Faluda)

Serves 4-6 people

**Ingredients**

2 cups milk

handful of china grass

3 tbsps sugar or to your taste

1 tsp rose water essence

a few drops of food colouring

1/4 cup water

**Method**

Soak the china grass in 1/4 cup of water for 15 minutes. Add the milk and sugar and let it simmer over a low heat for 10 minutes until the china grass has dissolved. Add the rose water essence and a few drops of colouring. Pour this into individual bowls. When cool, let it set in the refrigerator.

## Floating Island pudding (Tinga Tinga)

Serves 6 people

**Ingredients**

6 eggs

2 cups milk

1/2 cup sugar

1/2 tsp ground cardamom

1 tbsp custard powder

1/2 tsp vanilla essence

1 tbsp coarsely ground almonds

**Method**

Separate the egg white carefully and whisk very vigorously until stiff. Place the egg white on a plate. Boil water in a large saucepan and transfer the egg white onto the surface of the boiling water and cook for 7 to 10 minutes. Boil the milk and sugar in a saucepan over a low heat. Whisk the egg yolks and dissolve the custard powder in the yolks. Add to the milk mixture gradually whilst whisking. Add the cardamom and vanilla essence, and cook over a low heat stirring continuously until thickened. Transfer the cooked custard into a serving bowl and place the cooked egg white onto the custard and garnish with ground almonds. Serve cold.

## Coconut ice Cream (Ice cream ya nazi)

Serves 6-8 people

**Ingredients**

1 14 oz can coconut milk

1 14 oz can condensed milk

1 14 oz can evaporated milk

1 tsp grated nutmeg Or cardamom powder

1 tsp rose water essence

shredded coconut and mint to garnish

**Method**

Mix all the ingredients in a large bowl and freeze until ice crystals begin to form. Remove from the freezer and whisk until the mixture is fluffy. Put the mixture in a container with a cover and freeze until solid. Remove the ice cream 10 minutes before serving to allow it to soften. Garnish with shredded coconut and a sprig of mint

**Left:** Faludo dessert

# Bread

These different kinds of bread can be served alongside main dishes.

## Sesame bread (Mkate wa ufuta)

Serves 6-8 people
A speciality of Zanzibaris.

**Ingredients**

2 lbs plain white flour
1 sachet yeast
2 cups coconut milk
2 eggs
2 tbsps sesame seeds
salt to taste

**Method**

Sieve the flour into a bowl and add all the ingredients except the sesame seeds. Mix and knead to make a smooth dough. Cover and leave in a warm place to rise for half an hour. Divide the dough into small balls. Pat each ball into a round shape between the palms of your hand and then pull one side to make a teardrop shape. Sprinkle with sesame seeds and cook lightly on both sided under a grill or on a griddle.

## Chapatis

Serves 6 people
An international favourite.

**Ingredients**

8 oz chapati flour
1/2 tsp salt
1 tbsp oil
warm water to bind dough
margarine or butter for spreading

**Method**

Sift the flour and salt into a bowl. Add the oil and mix into a dough with sufficient warm water. Knead until soft and smooth. Cover with a damp cloth for 1/2 an hour. Knead the dough again and make into small balls. Dust a little flour on a board and roll the dough into a flat pancake about 3" in diameter. Heat a frying pan or a griddle and grill until it begins to puff up. Press with a spatula or with a cloth to assist the puffing process. Turn over and repeat the process. Remove from the pan and spread margarine or butter on the top. Cover in foil and serve immediately with vegetable or meat curry.

## Savoury pancakes (Mkate wa maji)

Serves 6 people

**Ingredients**

1 1/2 lbs wheat flour
1 onion chopped
2 eggs
salt to taste
oil for frying

**Method**

Bind the flour with two the eggs, chopped onion, salt and water. The dough should be soft like porridge. Heat a spoonful of oil in a frying pan and pour in one ladleful of the mixture. Lower the heat and let it cook until the pancake turns golden brown. Add a spoonful of oil and turn it over until the other side is cooked .Serve with a stew or curry.

## Coconut milk chapati (Chapati ya nazi)

Serves 4-6 people

**Ingredients**

4 cups plain white flour
1 cup coconut milk
1/2 cup oil
1/2 tsp salt

**Method**

Sift the flour and salt into a bowl. Add the oil and coconut milk and mix into a dough, adding warm water if necessary. Knead until soft and smooth. Cover with a damp cloth for half an hour. Divide the dough into 8 balls. Dust a little flour on a board and roll the dough into a flat pancake about 3 diameter. Brush a little oil onto the circle and dust a little flour and roll into a sausage, then coil into a round wheel. Roll out once more into a thin chapati. Brush oil on one side and fry until golden brown and repeat with the otherside. Serve hot with meat or chicken.

**Left:** Sesame bread

# Sauces, Relishes Pickles & Jam

## Zanzibari sauce (Rojo)

**Ingredients**

1 tbsp flour

2 cups water

1/4 tsp turmeric

1/4 tsp red chilli powder

1 small unripe mango or

juice of 1 lemon

salt

**Method**

Peel the mango and cut into small pieces and boil in very little water. When cool blend it and keep aside. Mix all the ingredients and boil, stirring continuously. Add mango pulp or lemon juice and cook for 1 minute. Serve with boiled potatoes, barbecued meat or on bhajias.

## Chilli tomato sauce (Pilipili tomato sauce)

**Ingredients**

1/2 cup tomato sauce

fresh red chillies or red chilli powder

lemon juice

salt

**Method**

Mix all the ingredients in a bowl and serve as a relish.

## Tamarind sauce (Chatni ya ukwaju)

Serves 6-8 people

**Ingredients**

1/2 cup tamarind pulp without stones

2 tsps red chilli powder

1 tsp salt to taste

2 tsps sugar

1 tsp jaggery (optional)

a few dates without stones

**Method**

Boil all the ingredients in 3 cups of water for 10 minutes. Allow to cool and blend in a food processor for 2 minutes. Squeeze all the pulp through a strainer. Tamarind sauce can be stored in the freezer.

## Coconut chutney (Chatni ya nazi)

Serves 6-8 people

**Ingredients**

1 fresh coconut or

8 oz desiccated coconut

1 small bunch fresh coriander

4 green chillies

1/2 tsp garlic paste

juice of a lemon

2 oz cashew nuts (optional)

pinch of sugar

salt to taste

**Method**

Blend all the ingredients with 1/2 cup of water until the mixture is very smooth. Serve with bhajia or as a relish.

## Onion salad (Kachumbari)

Serves 6-8 people

**Ingredients**

4 medium onions, sliced into thin rings

2 medium tomatoes chopped

1 small cucumber, peeled and sliced into thin rings

2 green chillies cut into very thin rings

juice of one lemon

salt to taste

**Method**

Mix all the ingredients together in a bowl and serve immediately.

## Raita (Mtindi)

Ideal for a summer's day, or as an accompaniment for curries.

**Ingredients**

1 carton natural yogurt

---

**Left:** Onion salad, Tamarind sauce, Coconut chutney, Raita, Zanzibari sauce and Chilli tomato sauce

1/2 tsp cumin seeds coarsely ground

1-2 green chillies finely chopped

1/2 cucumber finely chopped

coriander chopped

pinch of coarsely ground cumin to garnish

pinch of red chilli powder to garnish

**Method**

Mix all the ingredients together in a bowl and garnish with cumin and chilli powder.

## Lime pickle (Achari ya ndimu)

**Ingredients**

10 ripe limes

2 tbsps red chilli powder

1/2 tsp turmeric powder

1 tbsp salt

juice of 10 limes

**Method**

Mix all the spices with half the lime juice to make a paste and put the mixture aside. Cut the limes in quarters but not all the way so that the pieces stay together. Fill the limes with the paste. Put the limes in a sterile bottle. Add the remaining lime juice into the bottle and keep in a warm place for at least 3-4 weeks. Add more lime juice if necessary and occasionally shake the bottle.
Serve with rice and curries.

## Lemon Chutney (Chutney ya ndimu)

**Ingredients**

6 lemons

1 small piece of ginger shredded

2 tbsps sugar

1/4 cup vinegar

2 oz dates pitted

salt to taste

**Method**

Wash the lemons thoroughly. Cut into small pieces and remove the seeds. Mix the lemon pieces with the dates and all the spices and cook over a low heat until soft. When cool, bottle in sterile jars. Leave in a warm place for 2 weeks before serving.

## Pomelo salad (Saladi ya mbalungi)

Serves 4 people

**Ingredient**

1 large pomelo

4 tbsps sugar or to taste

1 tsp salt

1 tsp pepper

**Method**

Peel and remove the flesh from the pomelo and marinade in sugar, salt and pepper. Add sugar if necessary. Serve on a bed of salad.

## Tropical jam (Jam ya matunda)

**Ingredients**

1 orange

1 lemon

1 banana

1 small pineapple

1 small papaya

1 lb sugar

**Method**

Wash all the fruits, peel and core if necessary. Grate the rind of the orange and lemon and squeeze out the juice. Blend all the fruit. Put the grated rind, juice, sugar and the fruit pulp into a saucepan and bring to the boil slowly, stirring frequently until the jam thickens. Pour into a warmed screw top jar and close while the jam is still hot.

## Pineapple jam (Jam ya nanasi)

**Ingredients**

1 small pineapple

1 lemon

sugar to taste

**Method**

Peel and cut the pineapple into small pieces, add sugar and lemon juice and bring to the boil slowly, stirring frequently until the jam thickens. Pour into a warmed screw top jar and close while the jam is still hot.

**Left:** Lime pickle

# Index

Achari ya ndimu 93
Aubergine in coconut 57
Avocado whip 81

Baked bananas 85
Barbecued meat 47
Barbecued prawns 39
Bay leaves 19
Bean bhajia 65
Beans in coconut 57
Bhajia 63
Bhajia za dengu 49
Bhajia za kunde 65
Bhajia za batata 59
Biriani 75
Biringani wa nazi 57
Bitter tomatoes 55
Bokoboko 77
Bread fruit 51
Bungo juice (Rubber vine) 29

Caramel pudding 81
Cardamom 19
cassava 19
Cassava and beans 53
Cassava in coconut 51
Cassava leaf stew 51
Chai ya viungo 25
Chapatis 89
Chapati ya nazi 89
Chatni ya nazi 91
Chatni ya ndimu 93
Chatni ya ukwaju 91
Chicken and groundnut soup 33
Chicken in coconut sauce 45
Chicken kebabs 35
Chicken shashlik 61
Chila 73
Chilli 19
Chilli tomato sauce 91
Cinnamon 19
Cloves 19
Coconut chutney 91
Coconut doughnuts 71
Coconut ice cream 87
coconut milk 19
Coconut milk chapati 89
Coconut porridge 31
Coconut rice 75
Coconut squid 43
Coconut sweet 81
Coriander 19
Coriander leaves 19
Corn on the cob in coconut 59
Crab in coconut kaa wa nazi 41
Cumin seeds 19
Curry leaves 19
Cutlesi ya nyama 35

Cutlesi ya samaki 33
Dhal 20

Egg sweet/Mahsub 71
Exotic fruit drink 29
Faluda 87
Faluda dessert 87
Firni 83
Fish cakes 33
Fish in coconut 37
Fish Masala 37
Fish samosas 67
Fish soup 33
Floating Island pudding 87
Fried fish fillets 37
Fried squid 43
Fried vermicelli 85
Fruity coconut drink 27

Garam masala 20
Garlic 20
Garlic prawns kamba wa vitunguthomu 39
Ginger 20
Golden apple juice 29
Gram flour 20
Green bananas with beef or fish 49
Guava juice 27

Halua ya uwanga 81
Hot ginger drink 25

Ice cream ya nazi 87

Jaggery 20
Jam ya matunda 93
Jam ya nanasi 93

Kababu ya kuku 37
Kababu ya nyama 61
Kachumbari 91
Kahawa 25
Kaimati 73
Kamba wa kuchoma 39
Kamba wa salo 41
Kashata ya mayai 71
Kashata ya nazi 81
Khima mani 63
Kuku wa kuoka 45
Kuku wa kupaka 45

Lemon Chutney 93
Lemon grass 20
Lemon grass tea 27
Lentil bhajia 49
Lentils in coconut 51
Lime pickle 93

Mace 20
Maharagwe 57
Mahindi ya nazi 59
Maji ya mboga 29
Maji ya embe kizungu 29
Maji ya machungwa na embe 27
Maji ya matoufaa 29
Maji ya matunda na nazi 27
Maji ya mungunye na embe 29
Maji ya mastafeli 29
Maji ya papai na ndimu 25
Maji ya passion 27
Mahi ya ukwaju 25
Mandazi 71
Maridadi sherbati 29
Marrow and mango juice 29
Matunda salad 83
Mbaazi za nazi 55
Mbatata patties 61
Mbatata ya pilipili 61
Mboga 51
Mboga ya kisanvu 51
Mchai chai 27
Mchanyato 53
Mchicha wa nazi na karanga 53
Mchuzi wa choroko 51
Mchuzi wa nyama 47
Mchuzi wa nyama na mboga 45
Mchuzi wa mboga
Mchuzi wa papa 43
Mchuzi wa pweza 43
Mkate wa maji 89
Mkate wa ufuta 89
Mshikaki 47
Mshikaki wa nyama ya kusaga 69
Meat and vegetable stew 45
Meat curry 47
Meat kebabs 59
Meat pilau 75
Meat samosas 67
Meat with banana puree 47
Minced meat cutlets 35
Mint 20
Mixed bhajia 63
Mixed vegetable curry 47
Mkate wa kumimina 71
Mshikaki wa kuku 61
Mtindi 91
Mtori 47
Muhogo wa kuchoma 65
Muhogo wa nazi 51
Mungunye shuruba 83
Mustard seeds 20

Ndizi mbivu 85
Ndizi za kuchoma 57
Ndizi za Kuoka 85
Ngisi wa kukaanga 43

Ndizi mbichi ya nyama au samaki 49
Ngisi wa nazi 43
Nutmeg 20
Nyanya mshumaa 55

Octopus curry 43
Onion salad 91
Orange and mango juice 27

Papai la nazi 83
Papaya and lime juice 25
Papaya in coconut 83
Passion fruit juice 27
pepper-black 20
Pigeon peas in coconut 55
Pilau ya kamba 79
Pilau ya mboga 79
Pilau ya nyama 75
Pilipili tomato sauce 91
Pineapple jam 93
Pomelo salad 93
Potato patties 61
Prawn masala 41
Prawn Pilau 79
Prawn soup 31
Pudding ya mayai 81
Pudding ya peya 81
Pumpkin soup 31

Raita 91
Rice bread 71
Rice cakes 71
Rice flour dessert 85
Rice pancakes 73
Rice pudding 83
Roast sweet potatoes 55
Roasted Bananas 57
Roasted cassava 65
Rojo 67, 93
Rose apple juice 29

Saffron 20
Saladi ya mbalungi 93
Samaki wa kukaanga 37
Samaki wa kupaka 37
Samaki wa salo 37
Sambusa 67
Sambusa ya mboga 67
Sambusa ya nyama 67
Sambusa ya samaki 67
Samosa 67
Savoury pancakes 89
Savoury potato balls 59
Savoury spiced pancakes 65
Sesame bread 89
Sesame seeds 21
Sheli sheli 51
Sherbati ya mapera 27

Shishi kebab 69
Soft doughnuts 73

Soursop juice 29
Spicy chicken soup 31
Spicy potatoes 61
Spinach with coconut and peanuts 53
Stewed shark 43
Stiff porridge Ugali 77
Sugar syrup 21
Supu ya kamba 31
Supu ya kuku na karanga 33
Supu ya kuku viungo 31
Supu ya samaki 33
Supu ya tango 31
Sweet bananas in coconut 85
Sweet potatoes 65

Tamarind 21
Tamarind juice 25
Tamarind sauce 91
Tambi za nazi 85
Tambi za kukaanga 85
Tandoori chicken 45
Tinga Tinga 87
Tangawizi 25
Tropical fruit salad 83
Tropical jam 93
Turmeric 21

Uji wa nazi 31
Vanilla 21
Varango halwa 81
Vegetable pilau 79
Vegetable samosas 67
Vermicelli in coconut 85
Viazi vitamu 65
Viyazi vikuu vya nyama 49
Viazi vitamu vya kuchoma 55
Vipopo ya uwanga 85
Vitumbua 71

Wali wa nazi 75
Wheat and meat stew 77
White marrow milk shake 83

Yam and meat stew 49

Zanzibar coffee 25
Zanzibar lobster 41
Zanzibar mix 65
Zanzibar pizza 63
Zanzibar Spiced tea 25
Zanzibar kamba 41
Zanzibar sauce 65, 91

**Left:** Prawn masala

## ABOUT THE AUTHOR

**ZARINA JAFFERJI** was born in Zanzibar, and lived there in the Stone Town until she moved to the Uk in 1961 as a student. Her interests in flavours and recipes began naturally by entertaining people. Despite being based in Britain, Zarina has returned to Zanzibar several times a year, finding new recipes and witnessing the fusion of traditional Zanzibari cuisine with influences from Europe, the Middle East and Asia. She is dedicated to bringing Zanzibari's exceptional food to a world-wide audience, and ensuring that its cookery traditions are only enhanced, and not lost, in the Zanzibar of the 21st century.

The book contains over hundred temping recipes of a wide variety of Zanzibari dishes. Recipes are written with simple and easy to follow instructions, using ingredients which are ready available.

## ABOUT THE PHOTOGRAPHERS

**JAVED JAFFERJI** studied photography, film and television in the UK, before returning to Tanzania to publish various books, including Images of Zanzibar, Historical Zanzibar - Romance of the Ages, Zanzibar Stone Town - An Architectural Exploration, Tanzania - African Eden, Zanzibar Style, Zanzibar Style Recipes, Safari Living, Safari Living Recipes, Swahili Style, Swahili Kitchen, Safari Elegance and Safari Kitchen.

His work has been published in national and international newspapers and magazines. He has held exhibitions in London, Paris, Berlin and Pakistan as well as Tanzania.

Javed also publishes a magazine called 'The Swahili Coast' to promote coastal eco-tourism in Tanzania, manages a photography and graphic design company, and runs a shop, The Zanzibar Gallery, which sells gifts, clothes, books and antiques.

**PHILLIP WATERMAN** is a professional photographer based in London. He studied photography in Salisbury, England in 1991. He shoots people and fashion photos. His clients include top newspapers and magazines in the Uk. This project has allowed him to extend the variety in his work.